G000168639

Bank Regulation and the Use of Prompt Corrective Action

BANKING AND BANKING DEVELOPMENTS

Additional books in this series can be found on Nova's website under the Series tab.

Additional E-books in this series can be found on Nova's website under the e-books tab.

FINANCIAL INSTITUTIONS AND SERVICES

Additional books in this series can be found on Nova's website under the Series tab.

Additional E-books in this series can be found on Nova's website under the e-books tab.

BANK REGULATION AND THE USE OF PROMPT CORRECTIVE ACTION

DAVID GARCIA
AND
MARK J. HALL
EDITORS

Nova Science Publishers, Inc.
New York

Copyright © 2012 by Nova Science Publishers, Inc.

All rights reserved. No part of this book may be reproduced, stored in a retrieval system or transmitted in any form or by any means: electronic, electrostatic, magnetic, tape, mechanical photocopying, recording or otherwise without the written permission of the Publisher.

For permission to use material from this book please contact us:
Telephone 631-231-7269; Fax 631-231-8175
Web Site: http://www.novapublishers.com

NOTICE TO THE READER

The Publisher has taken reasonable care in the preparation of this book, but makes no expressed or implied warranty of any kind and assumes no responsibility for any errors or omissions. No liability is assumed for incidental or consequential damages in connection with or arising out of information contained in this book. The Publisher shall not be liable for any special, consequential, or exemplary damages resulting, in whole or in part, from the readers' use of, or reliance upon, this material. Any parts of this book based on government reports are so indicated and copyright is claimed for those parts to the extent applicable to compilations of such works.

Independent verification should be sought for any data, advice or recommendations contained in this book. In addition, no responsibility is assumed by the publisher for any injury and/or damage to persons or property arising from any methods, products, instructions, ideas or otherwise contained in this publication.

This publication is designed to provide accurate and authoritative information with regard to the subject matter covered herein. It is sold with the clear understanding that the Publisher is not engaged in rendering legal or any other professional services. If legal or any other expert assistance is required, the services of a competent person should be sought. FROM A DECLARATION OF PARTICIPANTS JOINTLY ADOPTED BY A COMMITTEE OF THE AMERICAN BAR ASSOCIATION AND A COMMITTEE OF PUBLISHERS.

Additional color graphics may be available in the e-book version of this book.

Library of Congress Cataloging-in-Publication Data

ISBN: 978-1-62081-149-8

Published by Nova Science Publishers, Inc. † New York

CONTENTS

PREFACE

The Dodd-Frank Wall Street Reform and Consumer Protection Act requires the Financial Stability Oversight Council to submit a report to Congress regarding the implementation of prompt corrective action (PCA) by the Federal banking agencies. This book discusses the existing PCA framework and the findings and recommendations of the Government Accountability Office study. It also highlights lessons learned from the financial crisis and outlines actions taken that could affect PCA, as well as additional steps to modify the PCA framework that could be considered.

Chapter 1- The Dodd-Frank Wall Street Reform and Consumer Protection Act (the "Dodd-Frank Act") requires the Financial Stability Oversight Council (the "Council") to submit a report to Congress regarding the implementation of prompt corrective action ("PCA") by the federal banking agencies.[1]

More specifically, section 202(g)(4) of the Dodd-Frank Act requires the Council to issue a report on actions taken in response to the GAO study required by section 202(g)(1) of the Dodd-Frank Act.

This report discusses the existing PCA framework and the findings and recommendations of the GAO study. It also highlights some lessons learned from the financial crisis and outlines actions taken that could affect PCA, as well as additional steps to modify the PCA framework that could be considered.

Chapter 2- More than 300 insured depository institutions have failed since the current financial crisis began in 2007, at an estimated cost of almost $60 billion to the deposit insurance fund (DIF), which covers losses to insured depositors. Since 1991, Congress has required federal banking regulators to take prompt corrective action (PCA) to identify and promptly address capital deficiencies at institutions to minimize losses to the DIF. The Dodd-Frank

Wall Street Reform and Consumer Protection Act requires GAO to study federal regulators' use of PCA. This report examines (1) the outcomes of regulators' use of PCA on the DIF; (2) the extent to which regulatory actions, PCA thresholds, and other financial indicators help regulators address likely bank trouble or failure; and (3) options available to make PCA a more effective tool. GAO analyzed agency and financial data to describe PCA and DIF trends and assess the timeliness of regulator actions and financial indicators. GAO also reviewed relevant literature and surveyed expert stakeholders from research, industry, and regulatory sectors on options to improve PCA.

In: Bank Regulation and the Use of Prompt ...   ISBN: 978-1-62081-149-8
Editors: David Garcia and Mark J. Hall © 2012 Nova Science Publishers, Inc.

Chapter 1

REPORT TO THE CONGRESS ON PROMPT CORRECTIVE ACTION[*]

Financial Stability Oversight Council

I. INTRODUCTION

The Dodd-Frank Wall Street Reform and Consumer Protection Act (the "Dodd-Frank Act") requires the Financial Stability Oversight Council (the "Council") to submit a report to Congress regarding the implementation of prompt corrective action ("PCA") by the federal banking agencies.[1]

More specifically, section 202(g)(4) of the Dodd-Frank Act requires the Council to issue a report on actions taken in response to the GAO study required by section 202(g)(1) of the Dodd-Frank Act.

This report discusses the existing PCA framework and the findings and recommendations of the GAO study. It also highlights some lessons learned from the financial crisis and outlines actions taken that could affect PCA, as well as additional steps to modify the PCA framework that could be considered.

---

[*] This is an edited, reformatted and augmented version of a Financial Stability Oversight Council publication, Completed pursuant to Section 202(g)(4) of the Dodd-Frank Wall Street Reform and Consumer Protection Act, dated December 2011.

II. PCA STATUTORY AND REGULATORY FRAMEWORK

The Federal Deposit Insurance Corporation Improvement Act of 1991 ("FDICIA") created the PCA framework embodied in section 38 of the Federal Deposit Insurance Act ("FDIA"). In accordance with the mandate of the FDICIA, the federal banking agencies conducted a joint rulemaking and adopted uniform rules to implement the PCA statutory framework. The federal banking agencies' rules established capital ratio criteria for the five capital categories under the statutory PCA framework and set forth the mandatory and discretionary actions for the agencies to address problems of banks in each capital category.

Under the statutory PCA framework the federal banking agencies are charged with the identification of problems of financially troubled banks at an early stage. The boards of directors and management of financially troubled banks are required to take prompt action as directed by the relevant agencies to remedy identified deficiencies.

The PCA framework includes five capital categories keyed to the federal banking agencies' current risk-based and leverage capital requirements. [2] The PCA framework provides more stringent mandatory and discretionary actions to be taken by the federal banking agencies in addressing the problems of a bank as it falls into lower PCA categories. The primary federal banking agency also is authorized to reclassify a bank to a lower PCA category, after notice and opportunity for hearing, upon determining that (i) the bank is operating in an unsafe and unsound condition or (ii) the bank received and has not corrected a less-than-satisfactory rating for any of the categories of asset quality, management, earnings, or liquidity.

Banks in any three of the less than adequately capitalized categories are subject to the provisions of section 38 of the FDIA restricting payment of management fees, requiring submission of a capital restoration plan, restricting growth, and requiring prior approval of certain expansion proposals. A bank that is significantly undercapitalized or critically undercapitalized or shows other signs of deterioration also may be directed to recapitalize itself (for example, by raising additional capital or being acquired by another banking organization), replace its directors and senior officers, make certain divestitures, and restrict compensation paid to senior executive officers. In addition, if a bank is critically undercapitalized, the PCA framework generally prohibits the payment of interest on subordinated debt. Furthermore, no later than 90 days after a bank becomes critically undercapitalized, its primary federal banking agency shall either (i) appoint a receiver or (ii) require other action (for an extendable period up to an additional 180 days) that it determines, with the consent of the FDIC, better achieves the purposes of the PCA framework.

In accordance with the requirements of section 39 of the FDIA, the federal banking agencies adopted rules that set safety and soundness standards for criteria other than capital, including earnings, asset quality, compensation, and management. These rules provide authority for the federal banking agencies to require corrective action if a bank fails to satisfy one or more of these standards.

III. THE GAO STUDY

Under section 202(g)(1)-(3) of the Dodd-Frank Act, the GAO must conduct a study regarding the implementation of PCA by the federal banking agencies.

The GAO study must evaluate ways to make PCA a more effective tool to resolve insured depository institutions at the least possible long-term cost to the Deposit Insurance Fund (—DIF), the effectiveness of implementation of PCA by the appropriate federal banking agencies, and the resolution of insured depository institutions by the FDIC.

The GAO study, released in June 2011, concluded that the existing PCA framework did not prevent widespread losses to the DIF, and that losses to the DIF as a result of the failure of banks that were subjected to PCA enforcement actions before failure were comparable as a percentage of assets to the losses of failed banks that were not subjected to PCA enforcement actions. The GAO study notes that —[c]apital can lag behind other indicators of bank health,‖[3] and, in light of this and other aspects of the PCA framework, the GAO recommends that alternative PCA triggers be considered, including indicators based on earnings, asset quality, liquidity, reliance on unstable funding, and sector loan concentration.

As part of the GAO study, the GAO surveyed various expert stakeholders. These expert stakeholders identified potential modifications to the PCA framework that could enhance its effectiveness, including (i) adding a measure of risk to the capital category thresholds, (ii) increasing the capital ratios that place banks into PCA capital categories, and (iii) adding an additional trigger. The GAO study acknowledges advantages and disadvantages associated with each of the potential alternative triggers identified and various challenges related to considering whether additional triggers or other enhancements could be developed.

To improve the effectiveness of the PCA framework, the GAO recommended that the federal banking agencies consider additional triggers that would require early and forceful regulatory actions tied to specific unsafe banking practices and also consider the other two options—adding a measure of risk to the capital category thresholds and increasing the capital ratios that place banks into PCA capital categories—identified in the GAO study. In considering such improvements, the GAO also recommended that the federal banking agencies should work through the Council to make recommendations to Congress on how PCA should be modified.

As the federal banking agencies have noted in their comments to the GAO study, future increases to the federal banking agencies' minimum capital requirements could lead to increased capital thresholds in each PCA category, and enhancements to these capital standards likely will be considered as the federal banking agencies implement capital requirements, consistent with the Basel 2.5 and III accords and the Dodd-Frank Act, as discussed below.

IV. LESSONS LEARNED DURING THE FINANCIAL CRISIS

As the GAO study points out, between 2007 and 2010, bank health deteriorated precipitously, as reflected by the rapid growth in and high number of banks on the FDIC's problem bank list and the number of troubled banks with CAMELS composite ratings of 3, 4 and 5. This period of stress in the banking sector tested the limits of PCA's effectiveness in a way not seen since PCA was introduced by the FDICIA. PCA is just one element that supervisors have been examining as they consider supervisory lessons learned from the financial crisis.

The GAO report and the responses of the federal banking agencies describe a number of supervisory enhancements already adopted or planned. In this vein, as regulators consider whether the PCA framework should be modified or enhanced, they will be working to implement a key lesson learned from the crisis – specifically, that the quality of capital and minimum capital requirements should be enhanced, as embodied in the Dodd-Frank Act, Basel 2.5 and Basel III.

Implementation of Basel 2.5, Basel III and the Dodd-Frank Act Enhanced Prudential Standards

In light of lessons learned from the crisis, the United States and other countries acting together through the Basel Committee on Banking Supervision (—Basel Committee") have developed more stringent capital requirements for internationally active banking organizations. Consistent with the federal banking agencies' comments to the GAO study, the agencies are in the process of developing rules to implement the enhanced capital standards adopted by the Basel Committee. These enhanced capital standards were agreed upon by the federal banking agencies and other countries participating in the Basel Committee and were endorsed by the Financial Stability Board (—FSB") and the G-20. The standards are intended to ensure that banks have strong capital bases from both micro-prudential and macro-prudential perspectives.

Basel 2.5, adopted by the Basel Committee in mid-2009, addresses the capital shortfalls in banking organizations' trading books, as experienced in the financial crisis, by significantly increasing capital requirements for banks' trading activities and assets held in their trading books. Basel III, which was agreed upon by the United States and other members of the Basel Committee in December 2010, increases banks' required levels of common equity. When the new rules are fully phased in there will be a common tier 1 requirement of 4.5 percent of risk-weighted assets and a capital conservation buffer of 2.5 percent (7 percent in aggregate) of risk-weighted assets, also required to be satisfied solely with common equity less required deductions (e.g., intangible assets and deferred tax assets). In addition, Basel III improves the quality of tier 1 and tier 2 capital by excluding certain instruments that do not satisfy the prudential criteria set by Basel III. Furthermore, Basel III includes the first internationally applicable leverage ratio. Another major action of the Basel Committee and the FSB, as endorsed by the G-20, is the release of the framework for determining global systemically important banks (G-SIBs). Banking organizations designated as G-SIBs will be required to hold additional capital buffers equaling from 1 percent to 2.5 percent of risk-weighted assets, depending on an assessment of each G-SIB's relative global position.

In addition, Basel III requires earlier constraints on capital distributions if the capital conservation buffer is not maintained. The federal banking agencies are developing proposals to implement the various Basel capital reforms in the United States.

The FRB and FDIC indicated in their comments to the GAO study that the implementation of Basel III could affect the capital thresholds incorporated in the federal banking agencies' current PCA standards. Furthermore, the Dodd-Frank Act requires the FRB to adopt enhanced prudential standards for bank holding companies with total consolidated assets equal to or greater than $50 billion and nonbank financial companies designated by the Council for FRB supervision.

These standards cover various supervisory factors including risk-based capital requirements.

Evaluation of the Need for Modifications to PCA

A thorough evaluation of the PCA framework and consideration of the need for changes should take into account the enhancements to capital and prudential standards described above, as well as the PCA framework's effectiveness through the entirety of the cycle that began with the deterioration of bank health in 2007.

Thus, when indicators of bank health, like the level of troubled and problem banks, show significant improvement, the regulators should consider the effectiveness of PCA and other supervisory tools in the context of the complete business cycle and any new capital standards that have been implemented.

A review that takes into account these factors will be able to more fully measure the PCA framework's effectiveness in mitigating the effect of bank failures, and therefore will provide a better opportunity to consider potential enhancement options based on complete data.

In addition, section 166 of the Dodd-Frank Act requires the FRB to develop an early remediation regime for bank holding companies with total consolidated assets of $50 billion or greater and any nonbank financial companies designated by the Council for supervision by the FRB. Importantly, section 166 requires the FRB to include —liquidity measures, and other forward-looking indicators‖ in addition to regulatory capital in the early remediation framework.

While section 166 and the PCA framework are separate, implementation of new rules under section 166 could provide regulators with additional experience to inform potential modifications to the PCA framework.

V. THE COUNCIL'S ACTIONS SINCE THE RELEASE OF THE GAO STUDY

The Council has considered the recommendations made in the GAO study, and will provide a forum where the banking regulators can discuss potential future enhancements to the PCA framework that they may want to consider.

The Council is providing a forum for interagency consultation and coordination as the FRB develops an approach to implement the enhanced prudential standards and early remediation standards under the Dodd-Frank Act, and these new standards could provide valuable insights as regulators consider potential modifications to the PCA framework.

When evaluating potential modifications to the PCA framework for non-capital related triggers, the Council suggests that the federal banking agencies consider data available after the current cycle in the banking sector has shown sufficient improvement. Moreover, while regulators acknowledge the potential weaknesses in using capital as a measure for the PCA framework, the manner in which any modifications to PCA are constructed to include alternative triggers in addition to capital will need to be carefully considered to be successful, as the GAO study also recognizes. In developing any potential enhancements to the PCA framework, the Council believes that the following principles, which are reflected in the existing PCA framework, continue to be carefully considered:

- PCA triggers should be objective to provide predictability.
- PCA triggers and accompanying corrective action should serve to reduce the likelihood and cost of bank failures, and accordingly must be carefully designed not to speed a bank's descent into an otherwise avoidable failure.
- PCA triggers should be based on broadly applicable financial metrics that do not discriminate against banks in particular size categories, geographies or business models. For example, the PCA framework should be cognizant of the differences in asset-type, concentration, and risk management for community banks when compared to larger financial institutions.
- PCA should complement a supervisory approach that encourages banks to improve their condition before severe automatic supervisory actions are required.

- Measures used in PCA should continue to have an automatic element that can provide a backstop to the existing supervisory framework, with an aim of ensuring prompt action to reduce the likelihood and cost of bank failures.

Section 202(g) of the Dodd-Frank Act also requires the Council to report on any recommendations made to the federal banking agencies under section 120 of the Act. As of the date of this report, the Council has not made any such recommendations.

End Notes

[1] The federal banking agencies are the Federal Reserve Board ("FRB"), the Federal Deposit Insurance Corporation ("FDIC"), and the Office of the Comptroller of the Currency ("OCC").

[2] "Well capitalized" (equals or exceeds a 10 percent total risk-based capital ratio, 6 percent tier 1 risk-based capital ratio, and 5 percent leverage ratio); "adequately capitalized" (equals or exceeds an 8 percent total risk-based capital ratio, 4 percent tier 1 risk-based capital ratio, and 4 percent leverage ratio); "undercapitalized" (total risk-based capital ratio of less than 8 percent, or a tier 1 risk-based ratio of less than 4 percent, or a leverage ratio of less than 4 percent (3 percent for institutions with a CAMELS rating of 1 that do not evidence rapid growth or other heightened risk indicators)); "significantly undercapitalized" (total risk-based capital ratio of less than 6 percent, or a tier 1 risk-based capital ratio of less than 3 percent, or a leverage ratio of less than 3 percent) and "critically undercapitalized (a ratio of tangible equity to total assets equal to or less than 2 percent). Tangible equity is defined in the PCA rule as the amount of core capital elements under the federal banking agencies' rules plus cumulative perpetual preferred stock minus all intangible assets other than mortgage servicing assets to the degree included in tier 1 capital under the banking agencies rules.

In: Bank Regulation and the Use of Prompt ...   ISBN: 978-1-62081-149-8
Editors: David Garcia and Mark J. Hall   © 2012 Nova Science Publishers, Inc.

Chapter 2

BANK REGULATION: MODIFIED PROMPT CORRECTIVE ACTION FRAMEWORK WOULD IMPROVE EFFECTIVENESS[*]

The United States Government Accountability Office

WHY GAO DID THIS STUDY

More than 300 insured depository institutions have failed since the current financial crisis began in 2007, at an estimated cost of almost $60 billion to the deposit insurance fund (DIF), which covers losses to insured depositors. Since 1991, Congress has required federal banking regulators to take prompt corrective action (PCA) to identify and promptly address capital deficiencies at institutions to minimize losses to the DIF. The Dodd-Frank Wall Street Reform and Consumer Protection Act requires GAO to study federal regulators' use of PCA. This report examines (1) the outcomes of regulators' use of PCA on the DIF; (2) the extent to which regulatory actions, PCA thresholds, and other financial indicators help regulators address likely bank trouble or failure; and (3) options available to make PCA a more effective tool. GAO analyzed agency and financial data to describe PCA and DIF trends and assess the timeliness of regulator actions and financial indicators. GAO also

---

[*] This is an edited, reformatted and augmented version of The United States Government Accountability Office publication, Report to Congressional Committees GAO-11-612, dated June 2011.

reviewed relevant literature and surveyed expert stakeholders from research, industry, and regulatory sectors on options to improve PCA.

What GAO Recommends

GAO recommends that the bank regulators consider additional triggers that would require early and forceful regulatory action to address unsafe banking practices as well as the other options identified in the report to improve PCA. The regulators generally agreed with the recommendation.

What GAO Found

Although the PCA framework has provided a mechanism to address financial deterioration in banks, GAO's analysis suggests it did not prevent widespread losses to the DIF—a key goal of PCA. Since 2008, the financial condition of banks has declined rapidly and use of PCA has grown tenfold. However, every bank that underwent PCA because of capital deficiencies and failed in this period produced a loss to the DIF. Moreover, these losses were comparable as a percentage of assets to the losses of failed banks that did not undergo PCA. While regulators and others acknowledged PCA's limitations, regulators said that the PCA framework provides benefits, such as facilitating orderly closures and encouraging banks to increase capital levels.

PCA's triggers limit its ability to promptly address bank problems, and although regulators had discretion to address problems sooner, they did not consistently do so. Since the 1990s, GAO and others have noted that the effectiveness of PCA, as currently constructed, is limited because of its reliance on capital, which can lag behind other indicators of bank health. That is, problems with the bank's assets, earnings, or management typically manifest before these problems affect bank capital. Once a bank falls below PCA's capital standards, a bank may not be able to recover regardless of the regulatory action imposed. GAO tested other financial indicators, including measures of asset quality and liquidity, and found that they were important predictors of future bank failure. These indicators also better identified those institutions that failed and did not undergo the PCA process during the recent crisis. Although regulators identified problematic conditions among banks well before failure, the presence and timeliness of enforcement actions were inconsistent. For example, among the banks that failed, more than 80 percent were on a regulatory watch list for more than a year, on average, before bank failure. However, GAO's analysis of regulatory data and material loss reviews showed that actions to address early signs of deterioration were inconsistent and, in many cases, regulators either took no enforcement action or acted in the final days before an institution was subject to PCA or failed. Without an additional early warning trigger, the regulators risk acting too late, thereby limiting their ability to minimize losses to the DIF.

Most stakeholders (23 of 29) GAO surveyed agreed that PCA should be modified and identified three top options to make it more effective. The first option—incorporating an institution's risk profile into PCA capital categories—would add a measure of risk to the capital category thresholds beyond the existing risk-weighted asset component. The second option was increasing the capital ratios that place banks in PCA capital categories. The third most popular option was including another trigger for PCA, such as asset quality or asset concentration. Each option has advantages and disadvantages. For example, while an additional trigger could account for other factors often found to precede capital deterioration, it might be difficult to implement. Although stakeholders supported these broad options, they cautioned that the manner in which any option was crafted would determine its success.

ABBREVIATIONS

ADC	acquisition, development, and construction
CAMELS	Uniform Financial Institutions Rating System
C&I	commercial and industrial
CRE	commercial real estate
DIF	deposit insurance fund
DRR	Division of Resolutions and Receiverships
FDIA	Federal Deposit Insurance Act
FDIC	Federal Deposit Insurance Corporation
FDICIA	Federal Deposit Insurance Corporation Improvement Act
FSOC	Financial Stability Oversight Council
HHI	Herfindahl-Hirschman Index
IG	inspector general
OCC	Office of the Comptroller of the Currency
OLS	ordinary least-squares
OTS	Office of Thrift Supervision

PCA   prompt corrective action
SCOR   Statistical CAMELS Off-site Rating
SR-SABR   Supervision and Regulation Statistical Assessment of Bank
            Risk

June 23, 2011

The Honorable Tim Johnson
Chairman
The Honorable Richard C. Shelby
Ranking Member
Committee on Banking, Housing, and Urban Affairs
United States Senate

The Honorable Spencer Bachus
Chairman
The Honorable Barney Frank Ranking Member
Committee on Financial Services
House of Representatives

After the savings and loan crisis, federal regulators were criticized for failing to take timely and forceful action to address the causes of bank failures and prevent losses to taxpayers and the deposit insurance fund (currently and hereinafter referred to as the DIF).[1] In response, Congress passed the Federal Deposit Insurance Corporation Improvement Act (FDICIA) of 1991, which made significant changes to the Federal Deposit Insurance Act (FDIA).[2] In particular, FDICIA created sections 38 and 39 of FDIA to improve the ability of regulators to identify and promptly address deficiencies at depository institutions—banks and thrifts—and better safeguard and minimize losses to the DIF. Section 38 requires regulators to classify banks into one of five capital categories and take increasingly severe actions, known as prompt corrective action (PCA), as a bank's capital deteriorates. Section 38 primarily focuses on capital as an indicator of bank health; therefore, supervisory actions under it are designed to address a bank's deteriorating capital level.[3] Section 39 requires the banking regulators to prescribe safety and soundness standards related to noncapital criteria, including operations and management; compensation; and asset quality, earnings, and stock valuation.[4] Section 39 allows the regulators to take action if a bank fails to meet one or more of these standards.

Before 2007, PCA was largely untested by a financial crisis that resulted in a large number of bank failures. After the passage of FDICIA, sustained growth in the U.S. economy meant that the financial condition of banks was generally strong. For instance, as a result of positive economic conditions, the number of bank failures declined from 180 in 1992 to 4 in 2004. And from June 2004 through January 2007, no banks failed.

Since 2007, failures have increased significantly. In 2010, 157 banks failed, the most in a single year since the savings and loan crisis of the 1980s and 1990s. The 157 banks had combined assets of approximately $93 billion, costing the DIF an estimated $24 billion. Overall, more than 300 banks have failed since the current financial crisis began in 2007, at an estimated cost of almost $60 billion to the DIF to cover losses to insured depositors. During this time, the balance of the DIF has declined dramatically, becoming negative in 2009. As of December 31, 2010, the DIF had a negative balance of $7.4 billion. During this same period, beginning late in 2008, the federal government provided significant financial assistance to many financial institutions through the Troubled Asset Relief Program and other actions taken by the Federal Reserve System and FDIC to stabilize the U.S. banking system.[5] For example, regulators used certain *emergency* authorities to enable assistance to some large banks because in their view the failure of these institutions would have imposed large losses on creditors and threatened to undermine confidence in the banking system.[6]

The number and size of failures during the recent financial crisis have raised questions about the ability of PCA to help turn around troubled banks and minimize losses to the DIF. Section 202(g) of the Dodd-Frank Wall Street Reform and Consumer Protection Act (Dodd-Frank Act) requires GAO to study the federal regulators' use of PCA and report our findings to the Financial Stability Oversight Council.[7] The Dodd-Frank Act also requires that the Financial Stability Oversight Council report to the Committee on Banking, Housing, and Urban Affairs of the Senate and the Committee on Financial Services of the House of Representatives on actions taken in response to our report, including any recommendations made to the federal banking regulators. Specifically, this report (1) analyzes the outcomes of regulators' use of PCA on the DIF; (2) evaluates the extent to which regulatory actions, capital thresholds, and other financial indicators helped regulators to address likely bank trouble or failure; and (3) identifies options available to make PCA a more effective tool to prevent or minimize losses to the DIF.

To describe trends in and outcomes from the implementation of PCA, we analyzed banking data from regulators, including FDIC Quarterly Banking

Reports and the quarterly "problem" bank lists. We analyzed data on banks that underwent the PCA process, failed from the first quarter of 2006 through the third quarter of 2010 (i.e., from January 1, 2006, through September 30, 2010), or both, and identified their outcomes.[8] To determine the number of banks that produced losses to the DIF—including those banks that underwent the PCA process before failure and those that did not—we used the 2010 estimate of losses to the DIF from loss data obtained from FDIC, which we determined to be sufficiently reliable for our purpose of enumerating failed banks and the losses associated with these failures based on our ongoing work related to the DIF.[9] We also interviewed representatives from FDIC, the Board of Governors of the Federal Reserve System (Federal Reserve), the Office of the Comptroller of the Currency (OCC), and the Office of Thrift Supervision (OTS).

To assess the utility of various financial indicators in predicting bank distress, we developed a model of leading indicators of bank failure based on financial ratios researchers identified in the 1990s that predicted bank failures in previous stress periods. We used these financial ratios, regulatory ratings, and an indicator we developed of sector loan concentration to forecast bank failure within 1 to 2 years (for failed banks and peers from 2006 through the third quarter of 2010). We used this model to assess the predictive power of indicators other than bank capital. To do this, we relied on data from FDIC and SNL Financial. We assessed the reliability of data used in our analysis and found the data sufficiently reliable for our purposes.

To examine the extent to which various regulatory activities and enforcement actions, including PCA, detected and addressed troubled banks, we examined the type and timing of regulatory actions across the oversight cycle. This work encompassed analyzing the extent to which existing regulatory steps provided warning of likely bank deterioration or failure. Specifically, we reviewed off-site monitoring tools and examined if these tools provided effective warnings of bank distress. For all bank failures that occurred from the first quarter of 2006 through the third quarter of 2010, we also reviewed formal and informal enforcement actions in the 2-year period before a bank failed to identify the earliest enforcement action taken in relation to other regulatory milestones associated with financial deterioration. We also reviewed the timing and nature of PCA enforcement actions in relation to bank failure. Upon receiving enforcement data provided by FDIC, the Federal Reserve, OCC, and OTS, we determined that the enforcement data provided could not be relied upon without additional verification. In particular, the enforcement data the Federal Reserve, OCC, and OTS provided could not be used alone to make distinctions among different types of enforcement actions that may or may not have been relevant to safety and soundness issues of banks that were deteriorating financially. While enforcement data provided by FDIC did make such distinctions, we did not rely exclusively on the enforcement data provided by the regulators, but rather, used these data to corroborate information on enforcement actions from material loss reports prepared by the inspectors general (IG) of the banking regulators and conducted case studies of 8 banks to highlight examples of oversight steps taken by each of the regulators and various outcomes. We selected a nongeneralizable sample of banks that is diverse with respect to geography, asset size, franchise value, primary regulator, date of failure, sequence of enforcement actions, outcome (failure or a return to financial stability), and losses to the DIF. The inspectors general for the FDIC, the Department of the Treasury, and the Board of Governors of the Federal Reserve System are currently conducting a joint evaluation of the PCA framework that will address the use of both sections 38 and 39 of FDICIA during the last few years, among other issues.

To identify options to make PCA more effective, we surveyed informed stakeholders from the regulatory agencies, research, and industry sectors. We used a two-part Delphi survey to gather ideas from the stakeholders, who were identified through professional credentials, authorship of research, and membership in relevant research and industry groups. The first survey, using open-ended questions, asked respondents to identify options, including those outside the PCA framework, which could be more effective in minimizing losses to the DIF. The second survey, through a set of closed-ended questions created from a content analysis of the responses from the first survey, asked the same stakeholders to rate and rank the options in terms of feasibility and impact. To further illustrate the options that may be considered to improve PCA effectiveness, we interviewed supervisory and research staff at the four regulators about PCA and bank failures during the financial crisis and any additional options that could improve PCA effectiveness. Finally, we conducted a literature review on PCA and early intervention and synthesized any additional options presented in the literature that could make PCA more effective. Appendix I contains a more detailed description of our scope and methodology.

We conducted this performance audit from July 2010 through June 2011 in accordance with generally accepted government auditing standards. Those standards require that we plan and perform the audit to obtain sufficient, appropriate evidence to provide a reasonable basis for our findings and conclusions based on our audit objectives. We believe that the evidence obtained provides a reasonable basis for our findings and conclusions based on our audit objectives.

BACKGROUND

Bank Supervision

Four federal regulators oversee banks and savings associations (thrifts) in the United States. The Federal Reserve is the primary regulator for state-chartered member banks (i.e., state-chartered banks that are members of the Federal Reserve System) and bank holding companies, OCC is the primary regulator of federally chartered banks, and OTS is the primary regulator of federally and state-chartered thrifts and thrift holding companies.[10] FDIC is the primary regulator for state-chartered nonmember banks (i.e., state-chartered banks that are not members of the Federal Reserve System). In addition, FDIC insures the deposits of all federally insured banks, generally up to $250,000 per depositor, and monitors their risk to the DIF.[11]

Regulators examine banks' risk management systems to help ensure the safe and sound operation of banks and protect the well-being of depositors—those individuals and organizations that act as creditors by "loaning" their funds in the form of deposits to banks for lending and other activities. Regulators are responsible for supervising the activities of banks and taking corrective action when their activities and overall performance present supervisory concerns or could result in financial losses to the DIF or violations of law. Losses to the DIF may occur when a bank does not have sufficient assets to reimburse customers' deposits and FDIC's administrative expenses in the event of closure or merger.

All the regulators assess the condition of banks through off-site monitoring and on-site examinations. Examiners use Report of Condition and Income (Call Report) and Thrift Financial Report data to remotely assess the financial condition of banks and thrifts, respectively, and to plan the scope of on-site examinations. Historically, banking regulators have used tools to monitor the financial condition of banks between on-site bank examinations. The off-site monitoring or surveillance activities rely largely on self-reported information from banks, filed through quarterly Call Reports to the banking regulators. Off-site monitoring and surveillance activities help alert regulators to potentially problematic conditions arising in a financial institution. Using these tools, each of the regulators identifies and flags banks with potential signs of financial distress for further regulatory scrutiny and prepares lists or reports of such institutions requiring further regulatory scrutiny (e.g., watch list, review list, high risk profile list, etc.).

As part of on-site examinations, regulators closely assess banks' exposure to risk and assign ratings, under the Uniform Financial Institutions Rating System, commonly known as CAMELS. The ratings reflect a bank's condition in six areas: capital, asset quality, management, earnings, liquidity, and sensitivity to market risk. Each component is rated on a scale of 1 to 5, with 1 being the best and 5 the worst. The component ratings are then used to develop a composite rating, also ranging from 1 to 5. Banks with composite ratings of 1 or 2 are considered to be in satisfactory condition, while banks with composite ratings of 3, 4, or 5 exhibit varying levels of safety and soundness problems. Banks with composite ratings of 4 or 5 are included on FDIC's problem bank list, which designates banks with weaknesses that threaten their continued financial viability. Also as part of the examination and general supervision process, regulators may direct a bank to address issues or deficiencies within specified time frames. However, as figure 1 illustrates, a bank's condition can rapidly deteriorate and bypass the various regulatory steps that usually occur as a bank's condition deteriorates.

When regulators determine that a bank or thrift's condition is less than satisfactory, they may take a variety of supervisory actions, including informal and formal enforcement actions, to address identified deficiencies and have some discretion in deciding which actions to take. Regulators typically take progressively stricter actions against more serious weaknesses. Informal actions generally are used to address less severe deficiencies or when the regulator has confidence that the bank is willing and able to implement changes.

Examples of informal actions include commitment letters detailing a bank's commitment to undertake specific remedial measures, resolutions adopted by the bank's board of directors at the request of its regulator, and memorandums of understanding that note agreements between the regulator and the bank's board of directors. Informal actions are not public agreements (regulators do not make them public through their Web sites or other channels) and are not enforceable by sanctions. In comparison, regulators publicly disclose and enforce formal actions. The regulators use formal actions to address more severe deficiencies. Formal enforcement actions include PCA directives, cease-and-desist orders, removal and prohibition orders, civil money penalties, and termination of a bank's deposit insurance.[12]

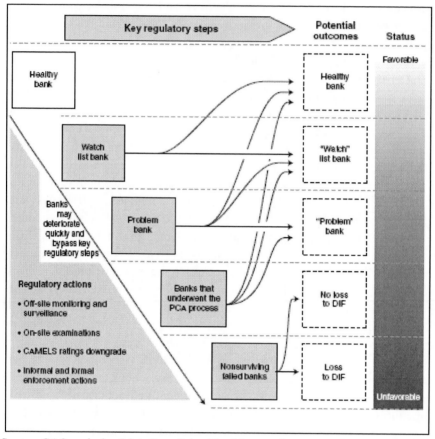

Source: GAO analysis of data from federal banking regulatory agencies.

Figure 1. Key Regulatory Milestones Associated with Bank Deterioration.

PCA

A principal goal of PCA is to prevent losses to the DIF for the vast majority of bank failures. Section 38 of FDIA requires regulators to categorize banks into five categories on the basis of their capital levels (see table 1). Regulators use four different capital measures to determine a bank's capital category: (1) a total risk-based capital ratio, (2) a Tier 1 risk-based capital ratio, (3) a leverage ratio (or non-risk-based capital ratio). The fourth PCA measure is a tangible equity to assets ratio for the Critically Undercapitalized category.[13] To be well capitalized, a bank must significantly exceed the minimum standard for all three capital measures. Depending on the level of deficiency, banks may be considered undercapitalized or significantly undercapitalized if they fail to meet any one of the ratios necessary to be considered at least adequately capitalized.

Table 1. PCA Capital Categories

Capital category	Total risk-based capitala	Tier 1 risk-based capital	Leverage capitalb
Well capitalizedc	10% or more and	6% or more and	5% or more
Adequately capitalized	8% or more and	4% or more and	4% or mored
Undercapitalized	Less than 8% or	Less than 4% or	Less than 4%
Significantly undercapitalized	Less than 6% or	Less than 3% or	Less than 3%
Critically undercapitalized	An institution is critically undercapitalized if its tangible equity is equal to or less than 2% of total assets regardless of its other capital ratios.e		

Sources: Capital measures and capital category definitions: FDIC—12 C.F.R. § 325.103, Federal Reserve—12 C.F.R. § 208.43, OCC—12 C.F.R. § 6.4, and OTS—12 C.F.R. § 565.4.

[a] The total risk-based capital ratio consists of the sum of Tier 1 and Tier 2 capital divided by risk-weighted assets. Tier 1 capital consists primarily of tangible equity (see note e). Tier 2 capital includes limited amounts of subordinated debt, loan loss reserves, and certain other instruments.

[b] Leverage capital is Tier 1 capital divided by average total assets.

[c] An institution that satisfies the capital measures for a well-capitalized institution but is subject to a formal enforcement action that requires it to meet and maintain a specific capital level is considered to be adequately capitalized for purposes of PCA.

[d] CAMELS 1-rated institutions not experiencing or anticipating significant growth need have only 3 percent leverage capital to be considered adequately capitalized.

[e] Tangible equity is equal to the amount of Tier 1 capital elements plus outstanding cumulative perpetual preferred stock minus all intangible assets not previously deducted, except certain purchased mortgage-servicing rights. Cumulative perpetual preferred stock is stock that has no maturity date, cannot be redeemed at the option of the holder, has no other provisions that will require future redemption of the issue, and provides for the accumulation or future payment of unpaid dividends. Intangible assets are those assets that are required to be reported as intangible assets in a bank's Call Report or thrift's Thrift Financial Report.

A bank that fails to meet the tangible equity to total assets ratio is considered critically undercapitalized. For example, a bank that is experiencing significant growth, with 9 percent total risk-based capital and 6 percent Tier 1 risk-based capital but only 3.5 percent leverage capital, would be undercapitalized for PCA purposes.

Under section 38, regulators must take increasingly stringent supervisory actions as a bank's capital level deteriorates. For example, all undercapitalized banks must implement capital restoration plans to restore capital to at least the adequately capitalized level, and regulators generally must close critically undercapitalized banks within a 90-day period.[14] Section 38 also authorizes several non-capital-based supervisory actions designed to allow regulators some flexibility in achieving the purpose of section 38. Specifically, under section 38(g) regulators can reclassify or downgrade a bank's capital category to apply more stringent operating restrictions or requirements if they determine, after notice and opportunity for a hearing, that a bank is in an unsafe and unsound condition or engaging in an unsafe or unsound practice.[15] Under section 38(f)(2)(F), regulators can require a bank to make improvements in management—for example, by dismissing officers and directors who are not able to materially strengthen a bank's ability to become adequately capitalized.

Section 39 directs regulatory attention to a bank's operations and activities in three areas aside from capital that also can affect safety and soundness: (1) operations and management; (2) compensation; and (3) asset quality, earnings, and stock valuation. Under section 39, if a regulator determines that a bank has failed to meet a prescribed standard, the regulator may require that the institution file a safety and soundness plan specifying how it will correct the deficiency. If the bank fails to submit an acceptable plan or fails to materially implement or adhere to an approved plan, the regulator must require the institution, through the issuance of a public order, to correct identified deficiencies and may place other restrictions or requirements on the bank pending the correction of the deficiency. We previously reported that regulators made limited use of their section 39 authority.[16]

Changing Condition of the Banking Industry

During the last few years, the condition of the bank and thrift industry has declined, particularly when compared with conditions in the relatively positive period beginning in the early 1990s following the passage of FDICIA.

Indicators of bank health, such as the number of banks on FDIC's problem bank list, show the deteriorating condition of banks since 2007 (see fig. 2). For example, in the first quarter of 2007, 53 banks were on the "problem" bank list, but by the third quarter of 2010, 860 banks were on this list. Moreover, the number of banks with CAMELS composite ratings of 1 and 2 has declined steadily since 2007 and 2008, respectively, and the numbers of 3, 4, and 5 ratings have increased over this period (fig. 3).

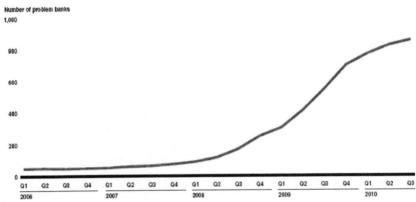

Source: GAO analysis of FDIC data.

Figure 2. Number of Banks on FDIC's Problem Bank List, First Quarter 2006 – Third Quarter 2010.

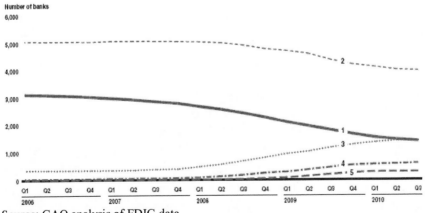

Source: GAO analysis of FDIC data.

Figure 3. Number of Banks by Composite CAMELS Rating, First Quarter 2006 – Third Quarter 2010.

Since the financial crisis began, the number of bank failures increased yearly from 2007 to 2010, with more than 300 banks failing during this time (see fig. 4). In 2010, 157 banks failed.

As a result of the rise in bank failures, the DIF balance has decreased dramatically (see fig. 5). Since the first quarter of 2007, the DIF balance has decreased by about $57 billion. The DIF balance was $50.7 billion at the start of 2007, hit a low point of negative $20.8 billion in the fourth quarter of 2009, and had a balance of negative $7.4 billion as of December 31, 2010.

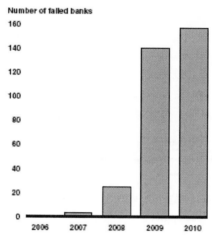

Source: GAO analysis of FDIC data.

Figure 4. Number of Failed Banks, 2006-2010.

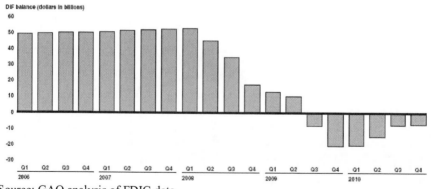

Source: GAO analysis of FDIC data.

Figure 5. Deposit Insurance Fund Balance, First Quarter 2006 – Fourth Quarter 2010.

PCA DID NOT PREVENT WIDESPREAD LOSSES TO THE DIF

Most Banks That Underwent the PCA Process Either Failed or Remained Troubled

As the recent financial turmoil unfolded, the number of banks that fell below one of the three lowest PCA capital thresholds—undercapitalized, significantly undercapitalized, or critically undercapitalized—increased dramatically. All four regulators told us that PCA was not designed for the type of precipitous economic decline that occurred in 2007 and 2008. As figure 6 illustrates, the total number of banks in undercapitalized and lower capital categories averaged fewer than 10 per quarter in 2006 and 2007, whereas the total averaged approximately 132 from 2008 through the third quarter of 2010.

The number of banks that entered the PCA process for the first time each quarter also increased dramatically. In 2006 and 2007, the number of banks newly entering undercapitalized or lower capital categories averaged fewer than 5 per quarter, compared with an average of 48 from 2008 through the third quarter of 2010 (see fig. 7).

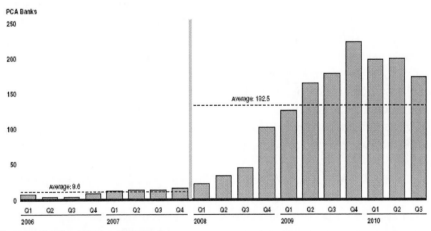

Source: GAO analysis of FDIC data.

Figure 6. Number of Banks That Underwent the PCA Process, First Quarter 2006 – Third Quarter 2010.

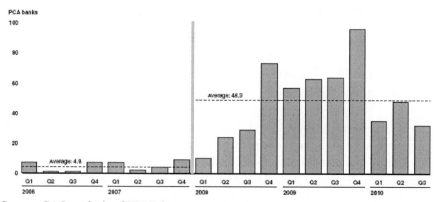

Source: GAO analysis of FDIC data.

Figure 7. Banks Undergoing the PCA Process for the First Time, First Quarter 2006 – Third Quarter 2010.

The vast majority of banks that underwent the PCA process from 2006 through the third quarter of 2010 had not returned to a condition of financial stability by the end of this period. As shown in figure 8, of the 569 banks that fell into the undercapitalized or lower capital categories of PCA, 270 failed. Another 25 banks failed without first being identified as falling into the undercapitalized or lower capital categories of PCA, bringing total bank failures to 295 during this period. Banking regulators told us that because of the sharp economic downturn in 2008, banks could deteriorate more rapidly than PCA was designed to handle.[17] For example, nearly half failed after being undercapitalized for two or fewer quarters. In addition, three regulators told us that early in the economic turmoil, banks that encountered sudden liquidity problems often did not trigger the PCA process before failure.

Although the remaining banks that underwent the PCA process did not fail, most of them continue to struggle financially. Specifically, 299 of the 569 banks that underwent the PCA process did not fail during the period of analysis.

Of these 299 banks, 223 remained undercapitalized or on the problem bank list through the third quarter of 2010 (see fig. 9). According to regulators and industry representatives, the large number of troubled banks may be due to sustained economic weakness during the period of analysis, which likely has hindered the ability of these banks to raise additional capital. Another 46 of the 299 undercapitalized banks were dissolved with minimal or no losses to the DIF.18 And the remaining 30 banks remained open and were neither undercapitalized nor on the problem bank list at the end of the period.

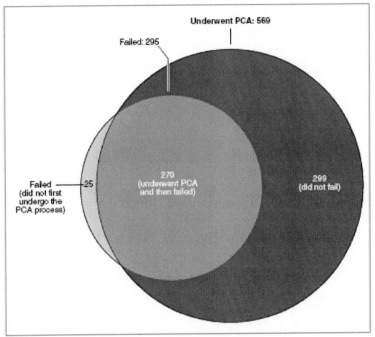

Source: GAO analysis of FDIC data.

Figure 8. Failures and Nonfailures of Banks That Underwent the PCA Process, First Quarter 2006 – Third Quarter 2010.

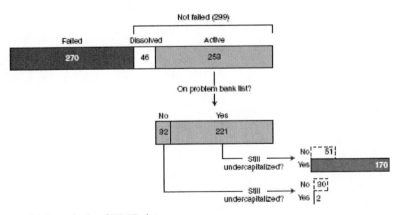

Source: GAO analysis of FDIC data.

Figure 9. Status of 569 Banks That Underwent the PCA Process, First Quarter 2006 – Third Quarter 2010.

All Banks That Failed after Undergoing the PCA Process Caused Losses to the Deposit Insurance Fund

Although PCA was intended to prevent or minimize losses to the DIF when banks failed, this goal was not achieved during the recent financial crisis. All 270 banks that failed after undergoing the PCA process during the period we reviewed caused losses to the fund, and these losses were comparable as a percentage of assets with those of the generally larger banks that did not undergo PCA. Thus, whether or not a bank underwent the PCA process before failure, its losses to the fund totaled approximately a third of its assets. Specifically, for banks that underwent the PCA process before failure, the minimum loss to the DIF as a percentage of assets was 1 percent, the median loss was 27.7 percent, and the maximum loss was 87 percent (see fig. 10). For banks that did not undergo the PCA process before failure, the minimum loss to the DIF as a percentage of assets was 0 percent, the median loss was 29.1 percent, and the maximum loss was 61 percent.19 However, after controlling for the financial condition of banks before they failed, we found that PCA had a small, positive impact on losses to the DIF as a percentage of assets. In particular, banks that went through PCA had losses that were 1 to 3 percentage points lower than those that did not undergo PCA before failure, but this difference was not statistically significant.[20]

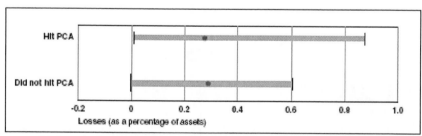

Source: GAO analysis of FDIC data.

Note: The mean loss to the DIF for banks that did not undergo the PCA process was 25.6 percent versus 28 percent for banks that did undergo the PCA process, though this difference was not statistically significant. After controlling for the financial condition of banks before they failed, we found that PCA had a small, positive (1-3 percent) impact on losses to the DIF as a percentage of assets, but the difference remained statistically insignificant.

Figure 10. Median Loss to the Insurance Fund of Failed Banks That Did and Did Not Undergo the PCA Process, First Quarter 2006 – Third Quarter 2010.

The 25 banks that failed without first being identified as undercapitalized or in lower capital categories generated losses that were larger in absolute terms, averaging $443 million compared with $246 million for the 270 banks that underwent PCA before failure.

However, the 25 banks that did not first undergo the PCA process tended to be larger—their median size, as measured by assets held the quarter before failure, was $372 million, versus $263 million for the 270 banks that underwent the PCA process.[21] In addition, our analysis suggests that the banks that did not undergo PCA before failure may have had characteristics that made them less likely to trigger the undercapitalized or lower capital thresholds of PCA because these banks may have possessed more capital. However, they also may have held fewer liquid securities or relied to a greater degree on unstable sources of funding, such as high-yield deposits from large financial investors.

Regulators Highlighted Benefits and Limitations of the PCA Framework

According to federal banking regulators, the PCA framework has provided them with a useful tool to address deteriorating banks.

Federal regulators told us that the PCA process is most effective in combination with other enforcement tools and it has multiple benefits in addressing financial deterioration in bank. They most frequently cited the following benefits:

- First, the PCA process may serve as a backstop or a safeguard to be used if other enforcement actions were delayed (for example, because a troubled bank contested a consent order).
- Second, the PCA program empowers state banking regulators to close critically undercapitalized banks—often in the face of significant pressure to forbear—and provides a road map for doing so.[22] Furthermore, officials from FDIC told us that state regulatory agencies had few occasions to close banks since the savings and loan crisis of the 1980s and 1990s, making such a road map more important because they could not draw on recent institutional memory of bank closures.
- Third, the 90-day closure provision in PCA facilitates an orderly resolution from the perspective of FDIC's Division of Resolutions and

Receiverships (DRR), which manages the closures of failed federallyinsured banks. FDIC DRR officials told us that the 90-day provision provides advance notice of a potential failure, enabling both FDIC DRR and potential buyers to conduct due diligence on the assets and liabilities of the deteriorating bank. According to FDIC DRR officials, the PCA advance notice results in higher bids for the failed bank. For more information on the resolution methods used to close failed banks, see appendix II.

- Fourth, the PCA framework encourages banks to hold more capital than otherwise would be the case. According to FDIC officials, banks often hold capital in excess of the required PCA capital thresholds to minimize the possibility of triggering mandatory supervisory action under section 38 of FDIA.

The banking regulators cited other benefits of PCA, including the specific authorities that section 38 affords. For example, OTS, OCC, and Federal Reserve officials said the ability to dismiss officers and directors from deteriorating banks was helpful, and FDIC officials said it was useful to be able to restrict the use of brokered deposits by banks categorized as adequately capitalized under the PCA framework.[23]

Regulators also noted that PCA increases consistency across the various regulatory agencies, which creates shared expectations about the process of monitoring, managing, and closing deteriorating banks. However, they emphasized that the effectiveness of PCA depended on making early and forceful use of their other enforcement tools.

Although regulators cited benefits of the PCA framework, they and industry groups also recognized several potential drawbacks of it. Some representatives specifically noted that PCA may discourage potential investors from investing in the troubled bank because of concerns that the bank's closure will wipe out their investment.

In addition, some officials and an industry group said that large banks with capital deficiencies are more likely to receive financial assistance or time to recapitalize than are smaller banks.[24] Finally, one industry group said that PCA is procyclical— that is, it magnifies the impact of wider economic trends on banks by compelling them to maintain, rather than draw down, their capital buffers. According to this industry group, by preventing banks from using their capital cushions, PCA hinders their ability to recover from financial distress.

OTHER INDICATORS PROVIDE EARLY WARNING OF DETERIORATION, AND ALTHOUGH REGULATORS IDENTIFIED CONDITIONS EARLY, RESPONSES WERE INCONSISTENT

Because they rely on capital, PCA's triggers have weaknesses, and the PCA framework does not take full advantage of early warning signs of bank distress that other financial indicators we tested can provide. Capital can lag behind other indicators of bank health, and once a bank's capital has deteriorated to the undercapitalized level, it may be too late for the bank to recover. Leading indicators of bank failure beyond capital—including measures of asset quality and liquidity—provided early warning of bank distress during the period we reviewed. Collectively, we found these indicators better identified those banks that did not undergo the PCA process before failure. Regulators generally were successful in identifying early warning signs of bank distress, but the presence and timeliness of subsequent enforcement actions were often inconsistent. While their off-site monitoring tools and CAMELS ratings often indicated deteriorating conditions more than a year before banks failed, regulators did not consistently take enforcement actions before banks underwent the PCA process.

PCA's Triggers Have Weaknesses

PCA's triggers have weaknesses in terms of initiating regulatory action upon early warning signs of bank distress. In the 1990s, several researchers at the bank regulatory agencies, as well as GAO, identified significant concerns associated with using the PCA bank capital thresholds to determine when to intervene in troubled banks. For example, one study found that capital is likely to trigger intervention after examiners already were aware of problems at a bank.[25] Another study found that most banks with a significant risk of failure in 1984-1989 (prior to the existence of PCA) would not have been considered undercapitalized under PCA.[26] Similarly, we have found that while capital was a valid measure of a bank's financial health, waiting until the capital standards have been violated may be too late for a bank to be able to address its problems. Banks had other identifiable issues before they were reflected in capital.[27] As discussed earlier we found that most banks that underwent the

PCA process either failed or remained on the problem bank list. Furthermore, nearly 1 in 10 banks failed without undergoing the PCA process.

Other Leading Indicators or a Composite Indicator Provided Early Warning of Bank Distress and Impending Failure

Other leading indicators, or a composite indicator, provided additional early warning of bank distress.[28] Several studies published in the 1990s demonstrated that in addition to capital, indicators based on earnings, asset quality, liquidity, and reliance on unstable funding provide early warning of bank distress. Capital on its own may provide some early warning of bank failure but does not capture weaknesses that manifest— perhaps earlier—in other areas of the bank's operations. We developed a model based on this earlier research to determine if these leading indicators would have been useful tools to predict bank failures during the current crisis.[29] As discussed below, our analysis confirmed that these same indicators (see table 2), as well as an indicator we developed based on sector loan concentration, would have provided early warning of problems in the banking system during this crisis.

Table 2. Select Leading Indicators of Bank Failure

Indicator	Definition	Explanation
Capital	Equity capital divided by assets	Measure of the net worth or solvencyof the institution
Earnings	Net income divided by assets	Measure of the profitability of the institution
Nonperforming loans	The sum of past due loans, nonaccrual loans, and real estate owned divided by assets	Measures the quality of loans (asset quality) held by the institution that may include losses not yet reflected in capital
Securities	Securities divided by liabilities	Measures the capacity of the institution to sell assets quickly to meet obligations
Unstable funding	Large ($100,000 plus) certificates of deposit divided by liabilities	Measures the reliance of the institution on certain high-cost and volatile funding sources

Source: GAO analysis of academic studies.

Note: We relied on two widely cited studies. See Cole and Gunther, "Separating the Likelihood and Timing of Bank Failure," and Cole and Gunther, "Predicting Bank Failure: A Comparison of On- and Off-site Monitoring Systems."

conditions in banks for further regulatory scrutiny (e.g., placing banks on watch or review lists).

In our review of 252 banks that failed from the first quarter of 2008 through the third quarter of 2010, most (82.5 percent) had been identified on review or watch lists within 2 years of their failure.[35] For these banks (regulated by FDIC, OCC, and the Federal Reserve), the median time between being placed on a watch or review list and failure was 631 days.

CAMELS ratings also provided early warning signs of bank failure. As described earlier, regulators formulate the CAMELS composite ratings using the individual component ratings, but the rating is not a mathematical average of the components. Individual component ratings may be lower or higher compared with the overall composite rating assigned. Any factor bearing significantly on the condition and soundness of the institution may be incorporated.[36] Banking regulators generally consider banks with a composite rating of 1 or 2 to be healthy, while banks receiving an unsatisfactory examination warrant a composite rating of 3 or above. We found that most banks that failed degraded from a CAMELS composite rating of 2 to a 4 in one quarter, though they generally had at least one component rating of a 3 prior to failure.

Specifically, among the 292 failed banks we reviewed (across all regulators), most (76 percent) received at least one individual component CAMELS rating of a 3 before failure.[37] At the same time, most (65 percent) also moved past the composite CAMELS 3 rating in a single quarter (e.g. moving from a 2 to 4) before failure, as the CAMELS composite ratings generally deteriorated precipitously. Our case studies of 8 banks also provided examples of this phenomenon, as banks frequently received multiple downgrades in the CAMELS composite ratings in a single quarter (see table 3 below).

For the failed banks that received either a CAMELS component or composite rating of 3, these ratings demonstrated the utility of CAMELS to provide early warning of bank distress. For example, among the failed banks that received a CAMELS component rating of 3, the median number of days between this component rating and bank failure was 459 days. Similarly, for failed banks that received a CAMELS composite rating of 3, the median number of days between banks receiving this composite rating and their subsequent failure was 508 days. In a separate analysis comparing peer and failed banks, we found that CAMELS ratings were useful leading indicators of bank failure. See appendix III for more information.

Table 3. Key Regulatory Activities and Milestones of Case Studies, First Quarter 2006–Third Quarter 2010

Institution	Watch/ review list	CAMELS 3 component	CAMELS 3 composite	CAMELS 4 component	CAMELS 4 composite	Problem bank list	Failed (as of 3/30/11)
1	12/31/07	12/31/07	DROP(2 to 4)	12/1/08	12/1/08	12/31/08	Yes
2	12/31/06	4/2/07	4/2/07	4/2/07	6/17/08	9/30/08	No
3	6/30/07	7/9/07	7/9/07	4/9/08	4/9/08	6/30/08	Yes
4	12/31/07	7/14/08	DROP(2 to 4)	7/14/08	7/14/08	9/30/08	Yes
5	N/A	4/10/06	4/10/06	1/29/09	1/29/09	3/31/09	Yes
6	N/A	1/1/06a	1/1/06a	11/13/07	3/17/09	3/31/09	Yes
7	1/1/06a	1/1/06a	1/1/06a	9/19/07	DROP(3 to 5)	3/31/08	Yes
8	9/16/09	10/1/09	DROP(2 to 5)	10/1/09	DROP(2 to 5)	12/31/09	No

Source: GAO Summary of data from FDIC, OCC, OTS, and Federal Reserve.
Note: N/A means not applicable.

institutions placed on a watch/review list prior to the beginning of our review period for this analysis, beginning January 2006.

While the Presence and Timeliness of Enforcement Actions Were Inconsistent, Regulators Have Incorporated Lessons Learned from the Financial Crisis

Although regulators generally were successful in identifying early warning signs of bank distress, the presence and timeliness of subsequent enforcement actions were often inconsistent. Most banks that failed had received an enforcement action (informal or formal) before undergoing the PCA process. The banking regulators told us that they typically issued enforcement actions to troubled banks—such as an informal enforcement action when a bank was downgraded to a CAMELS composite score of 3, and a formal enforcement action when it was downgraded to a 4—before these banks received a PCA directive. However, some banks did not receive any enforcement action before undergoing the PCA process, and many did not receive timely enforcement action prior to bank failure.

In our review of enforcement information available in material loss reviews or other evaluations on 136 failed banks, we found that the timeliness of enforcement actions was inconsistent.[38] However, we also noted that the timeliness of enforcement actions appeared to have improved during the banking crisis. Specifically, among 60 banks that failed between January 2008 and June 2009, approximately 28 percent did not have an initial informal or

In general, those key indicators identified by researchers in the 1990s are both statistically and practically significant predictors of bank failure during this crisis period (see app. III for more information).[30] Indicators of earnings, liquidity, and asset quality, in addition to capital, contain information about the condition of the bank that provides warning of bank distress up to 1-2 years in advance. For example, large differences in the level of nonperforming loans between healthy banks (our peer group) and banks that ultimately failed were evident well before the bulk of bank failures in 2009–2010 (see fig. 11). Starting in 2006, the difference between the two groups of banks increased as nonperforming loans grew dramatically over the next 3-4 years for banks that ultimately failed, but only modestly for healthy banks. Quantitatively, a one standard deviation increase in the level of nonperforming loans increased the chance of failure from roughly 2.8 percent to 7.8 percent over the next year.

Similarly, large differences in the level of liquid assets (securities) between healthy banks and banks that ultimately would fail are evident well before the bulk of bank failures (see fig. 12). The degree of liquidity fell somewhat over time, both at banks that ultimately would fail and healthy banks. Quantitatively, a one standard deviation increase in the level of securities decreased the chance of failure from roughly 2.8 percent to 2.3 percent over the next year. The Basel Committee has proposed two liquidity standards designed to promote resilience in the banking system.[31]

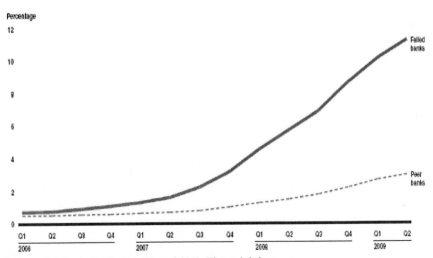

Source: GAO analysis of FDIC and SNL Financial data.

Figure 11. Nonperforming Loans (Asset Quality) at Failed and Peer Banks, First Quarter 2006–Second Quarter 2009.

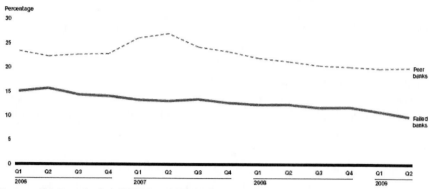

Source: GAO analysis of FDIC and SNL Financial data.

Figure 12. Liquidity at Failed and Peer Banks, First Quarter 2006–Second Quarter 2009.

As with indicators of earnings, liquidity, and asset quality, a measure of sector loan concentration we developed contains information about the condition of the bank that provides warning of bank distress up to 1–2 years in advance. Sector loan concentration is calculated as an index that incorporates the shares of an institution's loan portfolio allocated to certain broad economic sectors (e.g., residential real estate, consumer lending, etc.).[32] Our concentration index also proved to be an important predictor of bank failure— it is both statistically and practically significant (see app. III for more information). Banks that ultimately failed had considerably more concentrated loan portfolios than healthy banks well before the bulk of bank failures. Specifically, a one standard deviation increase in the degree of concentration increased the chance of failure from roughly 2.8 percent to 3.7 percent over the next year. Our concentration index partly reflects banks heavily invested in commercial real estate (see fig. 13)—a troubled sector during the recent downturn. Failed banks had roughly 20 percent more loans in commercial real estate than their peers. However, even among banks with the same degree of commercial real estate exposure, those with less diversified lending were more likely to fail. The concentration index we developed would be a more flexible forward-looking indicator than commercial real estate concentration alone because the next episode of banking stress will not necessarily be driven by commercial real estate.

The PCA framework does not take full advantage of early warning signs that financial indicators we tested can provide. Because PCA relies only on capital-based indicators, it may not capture institutional vulnerabilities that can

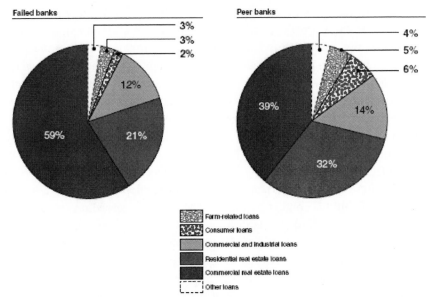

Source: GAO analysis of FDIC and SNL Financial data.

Figure 13. Loan Concentration at Failed and Peer Banks, First Quarter 2008.

manifest in, for example, limited liquidity, low asset quality, or high loan concentrations in particular sectors. Early warning signs in earnings, liquidity, asset quality, or concentration could be identified by assessing each indicator individually and setting indicator-specific thresholds. Later in this report we discuss indicators that could be used for triggers that respondents to our expert survey favored.

Composite indicators based on the model we developed or based on an existing regulatory tool (such as CAMELS ratings) provide a convenient way of combining information from a number of financial indicators, and can better identify risks in banks that did not undergo the PCA process before failure. Our analysis showed that a model incorporating these well-known leading indicators of bank distress better identified those banks that did not undergo the PCA process before failure—that is, the model placed them at a much higher risk of failure than healthy banks—than capital-based triggers alone. The average failure rate estimated by our model over the next year was about 20 percent for banks that ultimately would fail without triggering PCA (similar to the rate for all failures), and about 3 percent for healthy banks, as of the first quarter of 2008. Similarly, CAMELS ratings were higher (inferior) than ratings of peers at banks that did not undergo the PCA process before failure.

The CAMELS ratings were on average 2.13 for banks that failed without first undergoing the PCA process (similar to the ratings for all failures), and about 1.75 for healthy banks. While regulators use information from noncapital financial indicators in their supervision and off-site monitoring of banks, as we describe in the next section of this report, this does not always lead to timely enforcement action at problem banks. Two researchers also recently have suggested that PCA would benefit from the use of a composite indicator, such as those embodied in existing FDIC and Federal Reserve models, rather than only capital-based indicators.[33]

Regulators face a challenging trade-off between false positives (in this context, taking an action based on an incorrect prediction of bank distress) and false negatives (in this context, failing to take an action based on an incorrect prediction of bank health) in establishing a threshold or thresholds for capital or other indicators that might trigger intervention in potentially troubled banks. Striking the right balance between these two errors depends on the relative costs of each error, and other considerations. For example, the cost of acting on false positives could be quite high if healthy banks undertook costly and unnecessary measures to avoid regulatory triggers or similarly if regulators and banks expended significant resources during unnecessary interventions. Comparatively, the cost of failing to act on false negatives could be quite high if bank failures imposed dramatic costs on the DIF and the economy. In general, setting a high threshold for action only rarely would trigger unnecessary intervention in healthy banks but also might yield failures to intervene in some genuinely troubled banks. On the other hand, a low threshold would be more likely to trigger intervention unnecessarily in healthy banks but would correctly identify the bulk of troubled banks.

Regulators Used Tools other than PCA to Identify Early Signs of Bank Distress

All of the regulators used off-site monitoring or surveillance tools as well as CAMELS ratings to identify early signs of potentially problematic conditions among banks. In general, these regulatory tools, which incorporate assessments of bank characteristics beyond capital, provided early warnings of bank distress. For instance, FDIC and Federal Reserve models are key tools used for off-site monitoring or surveillance activities and contain many similar indicators of capital, liquidity, asset quality, and earnings.[34] As mentioned earlier, such models and other tools help regulators flag deteriorating conditions in banks for further regulatory scrutiny (e.g., placing banks on watch or review lists).

In our review of 252 banks that failed from the first quarter of 2008 through the third quarter of 2010, most (82.5 percent) had been identified on review or watch lists within 2 years of their failure.[35] For these banks (regulated by FDIC, OCC, and the Federal Reserve), the median time between being placed on a watch or review list and failure was 631 days.

CAMELS ratings also provided early warning signs of bank failure. As described earlier, regulators formulate the CAMELS composite ratings using the individual component ratings, but the rating is not a mathematical average of the components. Individual component ratings may be lower or higher compared with the overall composite rating assigned. Any factor bearing significantly on the condition and soundness of the institution may be incorporated.[36] Banking regulators generally consider banks with a composite rating of 1 or 2 to be healthy, while banks receiving an unsatisfactory examination warrant a composite rating of 3 or above. We found that most banks that failed degraded from a CAMELS composite rating of 2 to a 4 in one quarter, though they generally had at least one component rating of a 3 prior to failure.

Specifically, among the 292 failed banks we reviewed (across all regulators), most (76 percent) received at least one individual component CAMELS rating of a 3 before failure.[37] At the same time, most (65 percent) also moved past the composite CAMELS 3 rating in a single quarter (e.g. moving from a 2 to 4) before failure, as the CAMELS composite ratings generally deteriorated precipitously. Our case studies of 8 banks also provided examples of this phenomenon, as banks frequently received multiple downgrades in the CAMELS composite ratings in a single quarter (see table 3 below).

For the failed banks that received either a CAMELS component or composite rating of 3, these ratings demonstrated the utility of CAMELS to provide early warning of bank distress. For example, among the failed banks that received a CAMELS component rating of 3, the median number of days between this component rating and bank failure was 459 days. Similarly, for failed banks that received a CAMELS composite rating of 3, the median number of days between banks receiving this composite rating and their subsequent failure was 508 days. In a separate analysis comparing peer and failed banks, we found that CAMELS ratings were useful leading indicators of bank failure. See appendix III for more information.

Table 3. Key Regulatory Activities and Milestones of Case Studies, First Quarter 2006–Third Quarter 2010

Institution	Watch/ review list	CAMELS 3 component	CAMELS 3 composite	CAMELS 4 component	CAMELS 4 composite	Problem bank list	Failed (as of 3/30/11)
1	12/31/07	12/31/07	DROP(2 to 4)	12/1/08	12/1/08	12/31/08	Yes
2	12/31/06	4/2/07	4/2/07	4/2/07	6/17/08	9/30/08	No
3	6/30/07	7/9/07	7/9/07	4/9/08	4/9/08	6/30/08	Yes
4	12/31/07	7/14/08	DROP(2 to 4)	7/14/08	7/14/08	9/30/08	Yes
5	N/A	4/10/06	4/10/06	1/29/09	1/29/09	3/31/09	Yes
6	N/A	1/1/06a	1/1/06a	11/13/07	3/17/09	3/31/09	Yes
7	1/1/06a	1/1/06a	1/1/06a	9/19/07	DROP(3 to 5)	3/31/08	Yes
8	9/16/09	10/1/09	DROP(2 to 5)	10/1/09	DROP(2 to 5)	12/31/09	No

Source: GAO Summary of data from FDIC, OCC, OTS, and Federal Reserve.
Note: N/A means not applicable.

institutions placed on a watch/review list prior to the beginning of our review period for this analysis, beginning January 2006.

While the Presence and Timeliness of Enforcement Actions Were Inconsistent, Regulators Have Incorporated Lessons Learned from the Financial Crisis

Although regulators generally were successful in identifying early warning signs of bank distress, the presence and timeliness of subsequent enforcement actions were often inconsistent. Most banks that failed had received an enforcement action (informal or formal) before undergoing the PCA process. The banking regulators told us that they typically issued enforcement actions to troubled banks—such as an informal enforcement action when a bank was downgraded to a CAMELS composite score of 3, and a formal enforcement action when it was downgraded to a 4—before these banks received a PCA directive. However, some banks did not receive any enforcement action before undergoing the PCA process, and many did not receive timely enforcement action prior to bank failure.

In our review of enforcement information available in material loss reviews or other evaluations on 136 failed banks, we found that the timeliness of enforcement actions was inconsistent.[38] However, we also noted that the timeliness of enforcement actions appeared to have improved during the banking crisis. Specifically, among 60 banks that failed between January 2008 and June 2009, approximately 28 percent did not have an initial informal or formal non-PCA enforcement action until 90 days or less before bank failure. Further, 50 percent of these failed banks did not have an enforcement action until 180 days or less prior to failure. After June 2009, these percentages improved, with approximately 8 percent not having an enforcement action until 90 days or less before failure, and approximately 22 percent not having an action until 180 days or less before failure. Our case studies also provided examples of inconsistent enforcement actions. While some banks received an enforcement action before being subject to PCA, being placed on the problem bank list, or receiving a CAMELS 4 composite rating, others did not receive any enforcement action before these milestones. Table 4 highlights examples from our case studies of inconsistent regulatory attention tied to key regulatory activities and milestones. Furthermore, our findings related to presence and timeliness of enforcement actions were consistent with findings we reported in 1991.[39] Specifically, we found then that the banking regulators did not always use the most forceful actions available to correct unsafe and unsound banking practices.

Use of the current PCA mechanism as an enforcement tool was also inconsistent. As stated earlier, 25 banks (8 percent of the failed banks we reviewed) did not undergo the PCA process. For instance, in our case studies, we noted two institutions that were never subject to PCA prior to failure. For

Table 4. First Enforcement Action in Relation to Other Key Regulatory Milestones of Case Studies, First Quarter 2006–Third Quarter 2010

| Institution | Date | First enforcement action (non-PCA) | | | Initial PCA | Capital levelat initial PCA | Failed (as of 3/30/11) |
		Prior to CAMELS 4 composite?	Prior to problem bank list?	Prior to PCA?			
1	6/30/09	No	No	Yes	9/30/09	Undercapitalized	Yes
2	7/16/07	Yes	Yes	Yes	9/30/08	Undercapitalized	No
3	7/15/08	No	No	N/A	No PCA	N/A	Yes
4	8/25/08	No	Yes	Yes	9/30/09	Critically undercapitalized	Yes
5	1/8/08	Yes	Yes	N/A	No PCA	N/A	Yes
6	1/22/08	Yes	Yes	Yes	3/31/09	Critically undercapitalized	Yes
7	1/17/08	N/A	Yes	No	12/31/07	Undercapitalized	Yes
8	8/26/09	N/A	Yes	No	3/31/09	Significantly undercapitalized	No

Source: GAO Summary of data from FDIC, OCC, OTS, and Federal Reserve.
Note: N/A means not applicable.

those that were, the initial PCA capital category triggering enforcement actions frequently occurred at a more distressed capital threshold—significantly or critically undercapitalized—than the undercapitalized level. For instance, of the 270 failed banks we reviewed that underwent the PCA process, 40 percent were subject to an initial PCA enforcement action below the undercapitalized threshold, with 25.5 percent triggering PCA at the significantly undercapitalized level and 14.4 percent triggering PCA at the critically undercapitalized level. Figure 14 illustrates how PCA was used among 295 failed banks, including the initial capital thresholds triggering PCA enforcement actions. Similarly, our case studies provided examples of different initial capital thresholds that triggered PCA, including those occurring at the significantly undercapitalized and critically undercapitalized levels, as highlighted in table 4. Regulators have begun to incorporate a number of lessons learned from the financial crisis into their regulatory processes, including IG report findings. For instance, FDIC has developed and initiated training to be delivered in phases to reinforce and enhance its supervisory program. These efforts include identifying lessons learned from the results of the IG material loss reviews, emphasizing the importance of implementing timely and effective corrective programs, mandatory training for risk management and compliance examination staff to emphasize a forward-looking approach to examination analysis and ratings assessment activities, and providing enhanced guidance regarding supervision and examination procedures for de novo institutions.[40] At OCC, the Mid-Size and Community Banks Division issued a *Matters Requiring Attention Reference Guide* that provides examiners with OCC policy guidance on how to report, follow up on, and keep records related to Matters Requiring Attention. OTS has enhanced its Regulatory Action Data system to better flag matters requiring increased regulatory attention. We also noted that the Federal Reserve incorporated a new liquidity measure into its model used to identify banks that warrant being placed on its watch list.

WHILE MOST STAKEHOLDERS FAVORED MODIFYING PCA, THEIR PREFERRED OPTIONS INVOLVE SOME TRADEOFFS

Most of the informed stakeholders we surveyed told us the PCA framework should be retained but changed. We asked stakeholders from

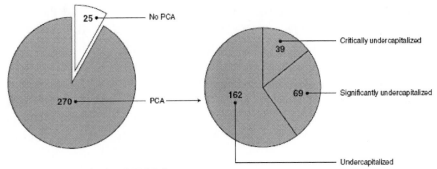

Source: GAO analysis of FDIC data.

Figure 14. Initial PCA Action of Failed Banks, First Quarter 2006–Third Quarter 2010.

research organizations, regulatory agencies, and the banking industry whether PCA should be changed and, if so, to identify and rank broad options to change the current framework to make it more effective in minimizing losses to the DIF. In response, 23 of 29 stakeholders said that PCA should be modified using one or more of the survey's listed options.[41] More specifically, they preferentially ranked three options—incorporating additional risk measures, raising capital thresholds, and adding an additional trigger—to make the PCA framework more effective. See table 5 for the full list of options in the survey and appendix V for full survey results. While each of these three options could improve the PCA framework, each presents certain advantages and disadvantages to consider. Furthermore, a few stakeholders emphasized that if PCA were modified, the specific details to implement such a policy change would determine whether the goal of minimizing losses to the DIF would be realized.

Incorporate an Institution's Risk Profile into the PCA Capital Category Thresholds

Stakeholders responding to our survey were most supportive of incorporating a bank's risk profile into the PCA capital category thresholds. Specifically, 12 stakeholders selected this option among the top three that should be considered, with 5 selecting it as their first option and 6 selecting it as their second option (see table 5). In addition, 21 of 29 stakeholders responded that incorporating an additional measure of risk into the PCA capital category thresholds would improve the effectiveness of PCA.[42] This option would add an additional risk element to the PCA capital measures beyond the already existing risk-weighted asset component.43 All four federal regulators told us that they can require banks to hold additional capital through formal or informal enforcement actions, but as noted earlier in the report, such actions are not always taken or the actions are not timely. Stakeholders suggested a few ways this change could be made. For example, in formulating the most appropriate capital thresholds, banks could be required to maintain an appropriate level of tangible equity or a capital buffer based on the level of risk-weighted assets.

Table 5. Rank Ordering of Survey Policy Options

Option to change the PCA framework	Number of respondents indicating option among top three that should be considered			Weighted score
	First	Second	Third	
Incorporate an institution's risk profile (concentration exposure, etc.) into the PCA capital category thresholds	5	6	1	28
Raise all capital category thresholds	7	2	1	26
Include an additional trigger for PCA (that is, another measure of bank soundness or performance)	3	4	5	22
Change accounting rules used to measure capital levels (make greater use of market values to assess assets, change rules for loan loss reserves, etc.)	3	3	1	16
Enhance restrictions and requirements at the holding company level	3	2	3	16
Make PCA restrictions and requirements less prescriptive (more flexibility in timelines, more discretion in application of restrictions, etc.)	4	1	1	15
Raise the critically undercapitalized threshold	2	3	3	15
Encourage greater uniformity across regulators (more consistency in capital definitions across state regulators and in closure authority across federal regulators, etc.)	0	3	5	11
Raise capital category thresholds for larger institutions	0	3	2	8
Eliminate the PCA framework	1	0	1	4
Strengthen PCA restrictions and requirements (shorter time frames, earlier use of restrictions available under the significantly undercapitalized category, etc.)	0	1	2	4
Make no changes to the PCA framework	0	0	0	0

Source: GAO.

Note: We calculated the weighted score by translating each respondent's ranking of
options into points: 3 points to a first choice, 2 points to a second choice, and 1
point to a third choice. The process of assigning weights to ranked preferences can
produce multiple outcomes. We acknowledge that alternate weights may change
the sequencing of the top three options.

Alternatively, specific risk areas such as liquidity or concentration could be factored into the determination of capital adequacy. Regulators already have the ability (on a case-by-case basis) to require banks to hold more capital than the amount required by PCA thresholds if they deem it necessary based on a bank's risk exposure.

Incorporate an Institution's Risk Profile into the PCA Capital Category Thresholds

Stakeholders responding to our survey were most supportive of incorporating a bank's risk profile into the PCA capital category thresholds. Specifically, 12 stakeholders selected this option among the top three that should be considered, with 5 selecting it as their first option and 6 selecting it as their second option (see table 5). In addition, 21 of 29 stakeholders responded that incorporating an additional measure of risk into the PCA capital category thresholds would improve the effectiveness of PCA.[42] This option would add an additional risk element to the PCA capital measures beyond the already existing risk-weighted asset component.[43] All four federal regulators told us that they can require banks to hold additional capital through formal or informal enforcement actions, but as noted earlier in the report, such actions are not always taken or the actions are not timely. Stakeholders suggested a few ways this change could be made. For example, in formulating the most appropriate capital thresholds, banks could be required to maintain an appropriate level of tangible equity or a capital buffer based on the level of risk-weighted assets. Alternatively, specific risk areas such as liquidity or concentration could be factored into the determination of capital adequacy. Regulators already have the ability (on a case-by-case basis) to require banks to hold more capital than the amount required by PCA thresholds if they deem it necessary based on a bank's risk exposure.

There are advantages and disadvantages to making this change to the PCA framework.

- *Potential advantages.* Adding an additional risk component to PCA capital measures may make PCA more responsive to specific trends. For example, in the current crisis many banks failed, in part, because of risks associated with high asset concentrations. A stakeholder told us that incorporating early indicators of heightened risk into PCA capital thresholds could be an additional way to minimize losses to the

DIF. Also, this change would not affect all banks but only those banks engaging in riskier activities. Moreover, incorporating a bank's risk profile into the PCA capital category thresholds would be an opportunity to broaden the scope of the PCA framework, helping mitigate the repeated concern among stakeholders that PCA, as currently constructed, is too narrowly focused.

- *Potential disadvantages.* This option could complicate the process of determining capital adequacy for PCA purposes, according to one stakeholder responding to our survey. For example, banks would vary in the levels of capital they needed to meet PCA capital thresholds, depending on their risk level. A stakeholder also cautioned that risk-based measures were complex and dependent on information from banks. Finally, adding a risk component to PCA could be duplicative because regulators already use risk-based capital ratios in PCA.

Raise All the PCA Capital Category Thresholds

Raising all the PCA capital category thresholds had the second-highest weighted score on our survey, and stakeholders selected it most often as a first choice. Specifically, 10 stakeholders selected this option among the top three that should be considered, with 7 selecting it as their first option (see table 5). In addition, 17 of 29 stakeholders told us increasing the capital category thresholds would improve the effectiveness of PCA.[44] This option would increase the capital ratios required for a bank to be classified as well capitalized, adequately capitalized, undercapitalized, significantly undercapitalized, and critically undercapitalized. Federal regulatory agencies have amended and updated the regulations and rules on measuring a bank's capital level in the past, often in conjunction with recommendations from the Basel Committee on Banking Supervision. However, the capital thresholds have not changed since the implementation of the PCA provisions of FDICIA in 1992.[45] The Basel Committee recently released guidelines recommending increased capital requirements to be phased in by January 1, 2015. Federal regulators typically adopt, with some national discretion, Basel Committee recommendations.

Raising only the critically undercapitalized threshold also was on our list of options. Twenty of 29 stakeholders we surveyed told us that raising the critically undercapitalized threshold would improve the effectiveness of PCA, more than the number who told us raising all PCA capital category thresholds would improve PCA effectiveness. However, when asked to select top options to improve the PCA framework, fewer stakeholders selected raising only the critically undercapitalized threshold. Currently, a bank is categorized as critically undercapitalized if its tangible equity is 2 percent or less. Regulators generally must close critically undercapitalized banks within a 90-day period.

Increasing PCA's capital category thresholds would change a nearly two-decades-old policy and involve trade-offs among the following advantages and disadvantages.

- *Potential advantages.* Raising thresholds would create an incentive for banks to increase capital levels. According to our previous work and the work of others, by holding more capital, a bank would have a greater capacity to absorb losses and remain solvent, particularly when a financial crisis occurred.[46] Similarly, with more capital, banks should be able to survive higher levels of borrower defaults. Thus, if banks were required to hold more capital, this might limit losses to the DIF in the event of failure by shifting risks from the DIF and taxpayers to the providers of capital, according to researchers. Moreover, increasing capital levels might not be a major change, as banks sometimes hold more capital than PCA requires.

- *Potential disadvantages.* If banks were required to hold more capital, they might change the way they conduct business. For example, banks might limit the amount of credit made available to businesses, households, and governments; charge higher interest rates on loans; or offer lower interest rates on deposits, according to researchers.[47] In addition, some banks might compensate for having less to lend by investing in riskier assets to seek higher returns. An industry group told us that raising the capital category thresholds could be particularly harmful for community banks, which often face additional challenges raising capital. A stakeholder told us this option also could create more instances in which regulators intervened in the operation of healthy banks (false positives)—that is, more banks may fall below a higher set PCA capital ratio standard even though they are not in financial distress. Additionally, 22 of 28 survey respondents said that PCA's focus on capital was a shortcoming of the process, and this option would not broaden the scope of PCA to other potential indicators of bank failure.

Add an Additional PCA Trigger

As their third preference, our survey respondents selected adding another PCA trigger. Specifically, 12 stakeholders selected this option among the top three that should be considered, with 3 selecting it as their first option, 4 selecting it as their second option, and 5 selecting it as their third option (see table 5). Overall, 18 of 29 respondents said this option would improve the effectiveness of PCA.[48] This option would require regulators to monitor other aspects of a bank's performance, such as asset concentration, asset quality, or liquidity, and if problems were identified, to take increasingly severe actions to address problems in that area. While regulators routinely monitor other aspects of bank safety and soundness, making these additional factors part of the PCA process would compel regulators to act when these areas were found to be deteriorating. However, as discussed previously in this report, we found that although regulators identified signs of bank distress, the timeliness of subsequent enforcement actions was inconsistent.

Stakeholders responding to our survey who recommended adding an additional PCA trigger were most supportive of using asset quality and asset concentration triggers. As discussed earlier in this report, our analysis of leading indicators of bank health found asset quality and asset concentration provided early warning of bank deterioration. When asked about the impact of an asset quality trigger, 26 of 28 survey respondents told us that it would improve the effectiveness of PCA.[49] Twenty of 29 survey respondents said an asset concentration trigger would improve the effectiveness of PCA. See appendix V for more information on how the survey respondents rated potential additional triggers.

Regulators have attempted to adopt additional triggers in the past. For example, regulators and a stakeholder with whom we spoke said that in the 1990s regulators tried to modify risk-based capital measures to account for asset concentration but were unable to develop a sufficiently reliable concentration metric. Instead, regulators decided to take risky asset concentrations into account during bank examinations. Additionally, FDIA (section 39) requires banking regulators to prescribe safety and soundness standards related to noncapital criteria, including operations and management; compensation; and asset quality, earnings, and stock valuations, allowing regulators to take action if a bank fails to meet one or more of these standards. Initially, the standards for asset quality and earnings were to be quantitative and intended to increase the likelihood that regulators would address safety and soundness problems before capital deteriorated. However, changes to

FDIA in the Riegle Community Development and Regulatory Improvement Act of 1994 gave regulators considerable flexibility over how and when to use their authority under the section to address safety and soundness deficiencies at banks.[50] After this change, we reported that section 39, as amended, appeared to leave regulatory discretion largely unchanged from what existed before the passage of FDICIA.[51] We also reported in 2007 that regulators made limited use of this authority, preferring other formal and informal enforcement actions.[52]

Including another PCA trigger could also produce advantages and disadvantages for regulators and banks.

- *Potential advantages.* Adding another trigger could mitigate the limitations of capital as an indicator. As we discussed in this and prior reports, regulatory actions focused solely on capital may have limited effects because of the extent of deterioration that already may have occurred.[53] Capital typically does not begin to decline until a bank has experienced substantial deterioration in other areas, such as asset quality and the quality of bank management. We previously recommended a "tripwire" approach to banking regulation, urging regulators to consider an array of factors such as assets, earnings, and capital deterioration and requiring banks to take specific actions to address problems in those areas.[54] We concluded that complements to capital standards such as industrywide measures for asset, management, and earnings conditions and a prescribed set of enforcement responses would improve the outcomes of the bank regulatory process.

- Potential disadvantages. Another trigger might duplicate other tools regulators already use in their supervision of banks, thereby creating inefficiencies in oversight. Also, the PCA trigger chosen might not be applicable to all banks. For example, one stakeholder cautioned that some triggers, such as asset concentration, sources of funding, and liquidity, might not apply uniformly to all banks.

Finally, a few stakeholders responding to our survey and experts with whom we spoke said that if PCA were modified, the specific details that shape the broad policy ideas would ultimately determine if the goal of minimizing losses to the DIF was realized. For example, some regulatory officials told us that in order for an earlier trigger to be effective, legislative changes would be needed to allow regulators to use the same authorities under the current PCA framework, such as the authority to dismiss bank officers and directors. Stakeholders also told us that the details matter greatly and how regulators ultimately crafted and applied the policies would determine if the policies were successful.

Before the current financial crisis, PCA was largely untested because the financial condition of banks generally had been strong since PCA was enacted. More than 300 bank failures later and despite some benefits in closing banks, the current PCA framework repeatedly has demonstrated its weaknesses for addressing deteriorating conditions in banks. In turn, PCA has not achieved a principal goal of preventing widespread losses to the DIF when banks fail.

CONCLUSION

Weaknesses in the current PCA framework stem primarily from tying mandatory corrective actions to only capital-based indicators. We and others have argued since 1991 that capital-based indicators have weaknesses, particularly because they do not provide timely warnings of bank distress. A number of alternative indicators exist or could be developed, and their advantages derive primarily from the early warnings of distress they could provide. In particular, a composite indicator can integrate information from a number of noncapital indicators in a single number. Regulators have stressed that the effectiveness of the PCA framework depended on making early and forceful use of other enforcement tools. However, while regulators have their own authorities and PCA also authorizes other discretionary actions, the regulators have not used these enforcement tools consistently. Tying mandatory corrective actions to additional indicators could mitigate these current weaknesses of PCA and increase the consistency with which distressed banks would be treated. And, enhancing the PCA framework in such a way would allow both regulators and banks more time to address deteriorating conditions. More important, banks facing such corrective actions likely would not be in as weakened a condition as typically is the case when current capital thresholds are triggered. Thus, the banks might have more options available to them to bolster their safety and soundness and avoid failure. Moreover, without an additional PCA trigger, the regulators risk not acting soon enough to address a bank's deteriorating condition, thereby limiting their ability to minimize losses to the DIF.

Expert stakeholders we surveyed also called for modifications to the PCA framework and identified several options for doing so. The top three options they identified include (1) adding a measure of risk to the capital category thresholds; (2) increasing the capital ratios that place banks into PCA capital categories and (3) adding an additional trigger. As the expert stakeholders noted and we also recognize, making any changes to the PCA framework would entail some trade-offs. Specifically, regulators would have to strike a balance between more corrective actions and unnecessary intervention in healthy banks.

The Financial Stability Oversight Council could provide a forum for vetting changes to the PCA framework and proposing these changes to Congress. Building consensus for potential changes, including working through the details of the changes and the associated trade-offs, will not be easy. But, in light of significant losses to the DIF in recent years, including at banks that underwent the PCA process, changes to the PCA framework are warranted.

RECOMMENDATION FOR EXECUTIVE ACTION

To improve the effectiveness of the PCA framework, we recommend that the heads of the Federal Reserve, FDIC, and OCC consider additional triggers that would require early and forceful regulatory actions tied to specific unsafe banking practices and also consider the other two options—adding a measure of risk to the capital category thresholds and increasing the capital ratios that place banks into PCA capital categories— identified in this report to improve PCA.

In considering such improvements, the regulators should work through the Financial Stability Oversight Council to make recommendations to Congress on how PCA should be modified.

AGENCY COMMENTS AND OUR EVALUATION

We provided a draft of this report to FDIC, the Federal Reserve, OCC, and OTS for review and comment. All of the agencies provided technical comments, which we considered and have incorporated as appropriate.

In written comments, FDIC, the Federal Reserve and OCC agreed with our recommendation to consider options to make PCA more effective. All three regulators noted that future enhancements to regulatory capital requirements could lead to raising the PCA capital category thresholds. FDIC and the Federal Reserve specifically stated that enhancements to capital requirements will likely be addressed when the regulators consider Basel III standards and that the PCA capital category thresholds could be impacted by rules implementing the Basel III standards. FDIC's written comments also reflected a concern regarding using noncapital based triggers for PCA and suggested such triggers "appear to have greater risk of unintended consequences" and should not be implemented without further study. However, the basis for FDIC's concern that triggers such as measuring concentrations, liquidity, management, or overall risk profile would pose greater risk of unintended consequences is unclear. As discussed in the report any changes to PCA require considering both the advantages and disadvantages. Our analysis demonstrated that adopting additional triggers within PCA also offers the potential for valuable benefits that must be considered. For example, our analysis demonstrated that noncapital triggers are more effective in identifying those banks that failed without undergoing the PCA process. The Federal Reserve also commented that one of the other options covered in the survey—changing accounting rules used to measure capital levels—but not discussed in detail in the report also offered promise in enhancing the effectiveness of PCA. As noted in the report, this was the fourth ranked option along with enhancing restrictions and requirements at the holding company level.

All three regulators noted in their written comments that they take supervisory enforcement actions in addition to PCA, as discussed in the draft report. Specifically, FDIC stated in its written comments that it had taken many supervisory actions in response to problems identified at the institutions it supervises and that it has strived to improve its supervisory processes based on lessons learned from material loss reviews. The Federal Reserve wrote that it did not find its supervisory enforcement actions to be inconsistent. OCC commented that it already imposes higher minimum capital standards for national banks whose risk profile warrants it. The enforcement action information presented in our report is compiled in aggregate from all of the banking regulators where material loss reviews or other evaluation reports were prepared subsequent to bank failure. However, we found examples from each of the regulators where no enforcement action (formal or informal) occurred until less than 180 days prior to bank failure. The material loss reviews for all of the regulators also commonly cited that earlier and more forceful supervisory action could have helped address deteriorating conditions earlier. We also noted in our report improvements over time in the overall timeliness of enforcement actions and that all of the regulators had taken actions to address previous weaknesses and lessons learned.

FDIC and the Federal Reserve also commented on the time period of our analysis. In written comments, FDIC noted that our results were "heavily influenced by the timing of the evaluation period" while the Federal Reserve similarly noted that because of the time period of analysis troubled banks had difficulty recovering due "to limited access to capital more than to the ineffectiveness of PCA." While we acknowledge that recent years have put considerable stress on the banking system, we believe that circumstances like this are critically important for assessing the performance of PCA—periods of bank distress are when PCA will be most seriously tested. In addition, changes to PCA based on options identified in our survey—such as higher capital thresholds—could assist banks in recovering during periods in which they have difficulty accessing capital from external sources.

A. Nicole Clowers
Acting Director
Financial Markets
and Community Investment

Thomas J. McCool
Director, Center for Economics
Applied Research and Methods

APPENDIX I: OBJECTIVES, SCOPE AND METHODOLOGY

Data Sources and Period of Analysis

To describe outcomes from and issues related to bank failures and losses to the deposit insurance fund (DIF), we analyzed quarterly data on the capitalization levels of federally insured banks from the Federal Deposit Insurance Corporation (FDIC). We obtained these data from FDIC Quarterly Banking Reports, which publish industry statistics derived from Reports on Condition and Income (Call Reports) and Thrift Financial Reports. All banks and thrifts must file Call Reports and Thrift Financial Reports, respectively, with FDIC every quarter. We have assessed the reliability of FDIC's Call and Thrift Financial Report databases as part of previous studies and found the data to be reliable for the purposes of our review.

Our period of analysis extended from January 2006, immediately after the ending point of our previous study, GAO-07-242, through the third quarter of September 2010. For this period, we calculated the total number of banks in any of the lowest three categories for prompt corrective action (PCA)—undercapitalized, significantly undercapitalized, or critically undercapitalized—in each quarter. We also calculated how many banks entered one of these capital categories for the first time in each quarter.

Our analysis excludes 13 institutions that received other assistance, such as assistance pursuant to systemic risk determinations. Although FDIC classified these banks as resolved, we excluded them because they remained operational.

Analysis of Bank Outcomes and Losses to the DIF

We reviewed bank failure data provided by FDIC to determine the number of banks that failed during our period of analysis, including their associated losses. We also reviewed data from FDIC that identified those banks that were subjected to PCA before failure and those that were not. We determined that the information from these datasets, related to DIF losses and capital levels from Call and Thrift Financial Reports, was sufficiently reliable for the purposes of our review based on ongoing and prior work using such data.

In addition, we used loss data from FDIC to identify the losses that each failed bank caused to the DIF failure, which we determined to be sufficiently reliable for our purpose of enumerating failed banks and the losses associated with these failures. We also analyzed losses to the DIF relative to the size of each failed bank.

To do so, we identified the total assets of each failed bank as reported on its Call Report or Thrift Financial Report in the quarter before failure. We used this measure and the losses that the bank caused the DIF (as estimated in 2010) to determine losses as a percentage of assets. To analyze the outcomes of banks in our analysis, we determined whether by the third quarter of 2010 a bank (1) had failed; (2) remained undercapitalized, was on the problem bank list, or both; (3) was dissolved; or (4) was not undercapitalized or on the problem bank list. We considered banks dissolved if they were not in the FDIC loss dataset or classified as active by FDIC by the end of this period. Many dissolved banks were merged into an acquiring bank without governmental assistance, although some were merged with assistance or were dissolved through a voluntary liquidation that did not result in a new institution.

Although components of these dissolved banks may have remained active, they operated under the certification number of their acquiring bank. We did not count banks as dissolved if they operated under their original certification number and FDIC classified them as active, regardless of whether a new entity had gained a large or controlling stake in their operations.

We used a number of econometric models to estimate the impact of PCA on losses to the DIF. We controlled for the financial condition of banks before they fail by holding constant factors affecting the quality of the balance sheet and the size of deposit liabilities. For more information, see appendix III.

We also interviewed officials from FDIC, the Office of the Comptroller of the Currency (OCC), the Office of Thrift Supervision (OTS), and the Board of Governors of the Federal Reserve System (Federal Reserve) to obtain their views on the effectiveness of PCA in minimizing losses to the DIF.

Analysis of Indicators, Enforcement Data and Case Studies of Deteriorating Banks

To assess the utility of various financial indicators in predicting bank distress, we developed a model of leading indicators of bank failure based on financial ratios researchers had identified in the 1990s that predicted bank failures in previous stress periods. Specifically, we used these financial ratios, regulatory ratings, and an indicator we developed of sector loan concentration to forecast bank failure within 1 to 2 years (for failed banks and peers from 2006 through the third quarter of 2010). We used this model to assess the predictive power of indicators other than bank capital. Additional information concerning the methodology for this analysis can be found in appendix III. To perform this work, we relied on data from FDIC and SNL Financial. We assessed the reliability of data used in our analysis and found the data sufficiently reliable for our purposes. To assess the regulatory enforcement actions associated with banks that had deteriorated, we examined the type and timing of regulatory actions for failed banks with various outcomes, and analyzed the extent to which regulatory indicators provided warning of likely bank deterioration or failure. To conduct this work, we requested enforcement data from FDIC, the Federal Reserve, OCC, and OTS. Upon receipt of this information, we determined that the enforcement data provided could not be relied upon for our specific analysis without additional verification. In particular, the enforcement data the Federal Reserve, OCC, and OTS provided could not be used alone to make distinctions among different types of enforcement actions that may or may not have been relevant to safety and soundness issues of banks that were deteriorating financially. While enforcement data provided by FDIC did make such distinctions, we did not rely exclusively on the enforcement data provided by the regulators. We determined that it was necessary to systematically pull relevant enforcement data on failed banks from material loss reviews and other evaluation reports prepared by the inspectors general (IG) of the banking regulators and corroborated this information with the enforcement data provided by regulators. Specifically, we reviewed material loss reviews and other evaluation reports available on 136 institutions that failed in 2008, 2009, and 2010. From these reports, we systematically identified the first enforcement action relevant to the regulator's efforts to address deteriorating conditions in a 2-year period before failure.

Further, we conducted case studies to explore supervisory, managerial, financial, and other characteristics commonly present in troubled or failed banks and illustrate the sequence of steps between the onset of trouble and a bank's closure. Specifically, we conducted case studies of eight banks to highlight examples of oversight steps taken by each of the regulators and various outcomes. For this work, we selected a nongeneralizable sample of banks that is diverse with respect to geography, asset size, franchise value, primary regulator, date of failure, sequence of enforcement actions, outcome (failure or a return to financial stability), and losses to the DIF. The case studies also allowed us to observe the off-site monitoring tools employed by regulators and examine whether these tools provided effective warnings of likely bank deterioration or failure.

Identifying Options That Could Improve PCA

To identify options that could help improve the effectiveness of PCA in minimizing losses to the DIF, we gathered ideas from a range of informed stakeholders from the regulatory, research, and industry sectors through a series of surveys.

We discuss the process used to identify stakeholders later in this appendix. We also conducted a literature review and interviewed agency officials and industry groups, and we incorporated the results into the survey process.

Delphi Survey Method

To gather options from informed stakeholders that could help improve the effectiveness of PCA, we employed a modified version of the Delphi method, which follows a structured process for collecting and distilling knowledge from a group through a series of questionnaires. For our purposes, we employed two iterative Web-based surveys.

Our first survey consisted of open-ended questions that asked respondents to provide their views on the positive aspects and shortcomings of the PCA framework, changes to the PCA framework that could make it more effective in minimizing losses to the DIF, and trade-offs associated with suggested changes to the framework. We conducted the first survey between November and December 2010.

We distributed a link for the survey to 44 individuals by e-mail and also subsequently e-mailed and telephoned nonrespondents to encourage a higher response rate.

We received completed surveys from 28 respondents (64 percent). Of the 28 completed responses, 17 were from regulators and supervisors, 9 were from researchers and consultants, and 2 were from industry participants. Of the 16 nonrespondents, 1 was an industry participant, 1 was a regulator and supervisor, and 14 were researchers and consultants.

On the basis of the 28 completed surveys, we performed a content analysis of the open-ended responses for all questions on the survey. We categorized the responses on the positive aspects and shortcomings into five categories each. We jointly analyzed the responses to the two questions asking about changes to or alternatives beyond the PCA framework and ultimately categorized the responses into 12 broad options.

To help ensure that our list of options for the second survey was thorough, we also reviewed literature on PCA and conducted interviews. We performed a literature search of studies (dating from January 2000 through October 2010) from major electronic databases, such as ProQuest and EconLit. We included studies that focused on PCA or reducing losses to the DIF in the U.S. financial system.

We only included studies that came from one of the following sources: peer-reviewed journals; federal regulatory agencies, GAO, Congressional Research Service, IGs; conference proceedings; advocacy and think tank organizations; or research institute, government, or think tank working paper series. We then reviewed the resultant studies to identify options that could improve the effectiveness of the PCA framework. In addition, we synthesized options that federal regulators, IGs, industry groups, and academics suggested during interviews. Overall, the literature review and interviews did not identify any broad options beyond those identified in the content analysis of the first survey.

However, we used specific examples for the options—specifically the option to include another trigger for PCA—from the literature review and interviews to supplement those gathered through the first Delphi survey. We also used the literature review and interviews to learn about trade-offs associated with options to change the PCA framework.

We conducted the second survey from February 2011 through March 2011. In our second survey, we asked recipients their opinion on the positive aspects and shortcomings of PCA identified in our analysis of the first survey. We also asked recipients to rate the potential impact and feasibility of the options to change the PCA framework and rank the three top options. We sent this survey to the same 44 individuals, and we sent out reminder Email messages and subsequently e-mailed and telephoned nonrespondents to encourage a higher response rate. We received completed surveys from 29 for a response rate of 66 percent.

Of the 29 completed responses, 15 were from regulators and supervisors, 11 were from researchers and consultants, and 3 were from industry participants. Of the 15 nonrespondents, 3 were regulators and supervisors and 12 were researchers and consultants.

Because of the number of nonrespondents who were from the research sector, the data collected from these surveys may not fully represent the views of this group.

Selecting Survey Recipients

We used a three-step process to determine which individuals would be invited to participate in our Delphi surveys. First, we identified the relevant sectors or groups of banking supervision stakeholders. We identified three sectors of stakeholders:

1) regulators and supervisors,
2) researchers and consultants, and
3) industry participants.

Next, we identified individuals within each of these sectors, through formal organizations when possible, including federal regulatory agencies, state regulatory associations, and industry groups. Our decisions to identify individuals were informed by the following criteria:

- professional credentials,
- authorship of research on PCA,
- testimony at relevant congressional hearings,
- membership in the Shadow Financial Regulatory Committee, and
- recommendations we received during initial interviews with industry groups and researchers.

When possible, we also consulted with organizations to confirm that we had identified the appropriate staff or member to include in our list of informed stakeholders.

To help ensure that our selection was thorough, we asked respondents in our first survey to recommend additional groups or individuals who they felt should be included.

Additional groups or individuals identified through this process were invited to complete both surveys based on the criteria described above. See appendix IV for a list of survey respondents.

Although we believe that this sample was sufficient for the purposes of identifying options that may improve PCA and for getting a sense of the relative impact and feasibility of these options, the survey was not a census of all informed stakeholders and was not given to a random, generalizable sample of stakeholders.

Therefore, the results represent only the views of the individuals who responded and are not representative of or generalizable to all informed stakeholders or all three sectors identified above. In addition, the practical difficulties of conducting any survey may introduce errors, commonly referred to as nonsampling errors.

For example, difficulties in interpreting a particular question, differences in sources of information available to respondents, or differences when analyzing data can introduce unwanted variability into the survey results.

We took steps in developing the surveys, collecting the data, and analyzing them to minimize such nonsampling errors. For example, we conducted a series of pretests with several survey recipients prior to distributing both surveys.

The goals of the pretests were to help ensure that (1) the questions were clear and unambiguous and (2) terminology was used correctly. We made changes to the content and format of both surveys as necessary based on the pretests.

APPENDIX II: THE RESOLUTION PROCESS ALSO CAN HELP MINIMIZE LOSSES TO THE DEPOSIT INSURANCE FUND

Beyond PCA, the selection of the bank closure method serves as an additional process for minimizing losses to the DIF. According to section 13 of the Federal Deposit Insurance Act (FDIA), the resolution method FDIC selects must be the alternative that is least costly to the insurance fund, except in cases involving systemic risk where FDIC may take other action for the purpose of winding up the insured depository institution for which the FDIC has been appointed receiver as necessary to avoid or mitigate such effects.[1] To select the least costly method, FDIC compares the estimated cost of liquidation—basically, the amount of insured deposits FDIC must pay minus the net realizable value of a bank's assets— with the amounts that potential acquirers bid for the bank's assets and deposits. The most common resolution method for failing banks is the purchase and assumption transaction, in which a healthy bank purchases certain assets and assumes certain liabilities of a failed bank. FDIC sells banks through a purchase and assumption transaction unless another approach is less costly to the DIF.

According to FDIC, their ability to influence the cost of bank failures to the DIF is limited, but FDIC said certain resolution methods helped minimize losses. FDIC's Division of Resolutions and Receiverships (DRR) told us that the cost of a bank failure to the DIF is embedded in the financial position of the failed bank. According to FDIC DRR, factors (beyond the resolution process) that affect the cost of a bank failure are both internal and external to the failed bank. For instance, the stability of the bank's funding sources—that is, the degree to which the bank has a stable base of customers rather than "brokered" or bulk deposits from out-of-state institutional investors—is a key internal factor. The quality of the bank's assets (for example, the proportion of its loans that carry a high risk of default) is a second, key internal factor. External factors such as wider economic conditions and the risk appetite of potential buyers also affect the cost of a bank failure.

FDIC DRR officials told us that although the cost of a bank failure is largely fixed by the time of failure, the manner of resolution can affect losses to the DIF "in the margin." In an effort to minimize these losses, FDIC DRR customized purchase and assumption transactions, which it used to sell 254 of the 270 banks that failed after undergoing the PCA process, to the needs of the market. In a purchase and assumption transaction, a healthy bank purchases certain assets and assumes certain liabilities of a failed bank. The specific composition of the transaction depends on the assets and liabilities held by the failed bank as well as wider market conditions. FDIC may offer to sell acquirers (1) the whole failed bank; (2) the whole failed bank with a shared-loss agreement, an arrangement whereby FDIC, with the intent of limiting losses to the deposit insurance fund, agrees to share with the acquirer the losses on those assets; (3) less than whole bank with a shared-loss agreement; or (4) a clean transfer (cash, securities, and insured deposits). FDIC DRR resolved the remaining 16 of the 270 banks that failed after being subject to PCA through direct payout, a scenario in which FDIC pays depositors directly and places the assets of the failed bank in a receivership.

Beyond tailoring purchase and assumption transactions to the needs of the market, FDIC DRR pursued strategies based on the rationale that the longterm intrinsic value of the assets of failed banks exceeded their depressed market value. Examples are the FDIC structured transaction program, in which FDIC acts as a receiver and partners with a private-sector institution to dispose of assets from failed banks. According to FDIC DRR, this program enables FDIC to take advantage of private-sector knowledge while recouping future cash flows from the failed bank. FDIC also sought to increase the value of distressed assets through a loan modification program. In this program, FDIC works with failed banks to modify rather than foreclose on residential mortgages. This reduces the number of borrowers who face foreclosure and rehabilitates inactive mortgages into performing loans.

FDIC DRR told us that it used shared-loss agreements to increase the value of distressed assets and protect the DIF. When market values were falling, in 2008, FDIC DRR's valuations of failed banks were too high to attract bidders. As its backlog of banks grew, FDIC DRR adopted a loss-share approach in which it sold a pool of problem assets to an acquirer under an agreement that FDIC would share a portion of the losses. This structure allowed FDIC to reduce the immediate cash outlays for the transaction. Figure 15 illustrates the increase in shared-loss agreements from 2007 through the third quarter of 2010.

According to FDIC, these shared-loss agreements enabled FDIC to transfer failed banks to a private-sector acquirer, an outcome that cost the fund less than liquidation of the failed bank.

FDIC DRR told us that as the economy improved in 2010, it received bids for failed banks that included no loss-share agreement. For shared-loss agreements that FDIC did offer in this time period, it shifted more risk to bidders. Because the losses to the DIF from these shared-loss agreements will

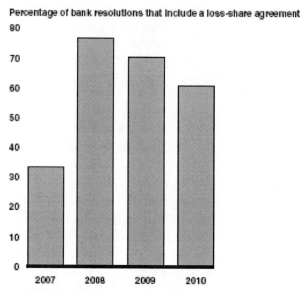

Percentage of bank resolutions that include a loss-share agreement

Source: GAO analysis of FDIC data.

Figure 15. Trends in Use of Shared-loss Agreements, First Quarter 2006–Third Quarter 2010.

be realized over longer time horizons (for example, 8-10 years), it is too early to thoroughly evaluate the relative merits of the shared-loss agreements against other resolution methods.

APPENDIX III: ECONOMETRIC ANALYSIS OF LEADING INDICATORS OF BANK FAILURE AND DETERMINANTS OF LOSSES TO THE DEPOSIT INSURANCE FUND

This appendix describes the methodological approach we took to identify potential leading indicators of bank failure, generate a peer group for the population of failed banks, and evaluate the statistical and practical significance of potential leading indicators during the current period of bank distress. The appendix also describes the methodology and results for assessing potential determinants of losses to the DIF and impact of PCA.

METHODOLOGICAL APPROACH

In order to construct a logistic (logit) regression model of bank failure prediction, we identified leading indicators from a previous period of bank failures based principally on two studies.[1] We selected the following five financial ratios: equity capital/assets, earnings/assets, nonperforming loans (sum of past due loans, nonaccrual loans, and real estate owned)/assets, securities/liabilities, and "jumbo" ($100,000 plus) certificates of deposit/liabilities. The rationale for each of these indicators is described in table 6 below.

We found that the equity capital measure from the literature evolved in a way that was quite similar to certain regulatory capital measures (see fig. 16) for banks that ultimately failed.

The correlation between the aggregate equity capital measure and the leverage ratio was 0.99; the correlation with the tier 1 capital to risk-weighted assets ratio was 0.97.

Table 6. Select Leading Indicators of Bank Failure

Indicator	Definition	Explanation
Capital	Equity capital divided by assets	Measure of the net worth or solvency of the institution
Earnings	Net income divided by assets	Measure of the profitability of the institution
Nonperforming loans	The sum of past due loans, nonaccrual loans, and real estate owned divided by assets	Measures the quality of loans (asset quality) held by the institution, which may include losses not yet reflected in capital
Securities	Securities divided by liabilities	Measures the capacity of the institution to sell assets quickly to meet obligations
Unstable funding	Large ($100,000 plus) certificates of deposit divided by liabilities	Measures the reliance of the institution on certain high-cost andvolatile funding sources

Source: GAO analysis of academic studies.

Note: We relied on two widely cited studies. See Cole and Gunther, "Separating the Likelihood and Timing of Bank Failure," and Cole and Gunther, "Predicting Bank Failure: A Comparison of On- and Off-site Monitoring Systems".

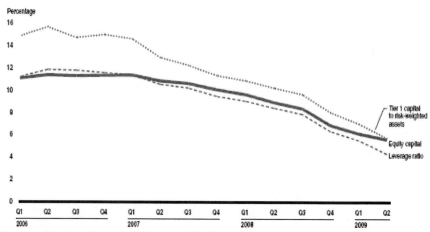

Source: GAO analysis of FDIC and SNL Financial data.

Figure 16. Equity Capital and Regulatory Capital at Failed Banks, First Quarter 2006–Second Quarter 2009.

Given the attention to commercial real estate concentrations during this crisis, we developed a more generic measure of loan concentration as a potential leading indicator. The Bank for International Settlements and Deutsche Bundesbank have described how a Herfindahl-Hirschman Index (HHI) could be used to measure loan concentration.[2] We adopted a version based on sectors defined below. This is an imperfect measure of concentration because it does not account for the correlations between the various sectors and with the overall economy. However, an HHI is a useful and straightforward indicator of credit concentration.

All else being equal, it should be associated with greater risk and there may therefore be associated with a greater likelihood of failure. We define two possible HHIs based on two different sector definitions (identical except for one distinction—in HHI 1 multifamily residential real estate is included with one-four family residential real estate, and in HHI 2 it is included with commercial real estate):

- *HHI 1:* Sector shares are defined as acquisition, development, and construction loans (ADC) plus nonfarm nonresidential real estate (commercial real estate, or CRE, narrowly defined), residential real estate (including one-four family and multifamily [five or more] real estate), consumer loans, loans to farms plus agricultural production loans, commercial and industrial (C&I) loans, and other (a residual).

- *HHI 2:* Sector shares are defined as ADC loans plus nonfarm nonresidential real estate (CRE narrowly defined) plus multifamily residential real estate loans (these three sectors are similar to the broad definition of CRE used in the joint CRE concentration guidance that the federal banking regulators issued), one-four family residential real estate loans, consumer loans, loans to farms plus agricultural production loans, C&I loans, and other (a residual).[3]

We identified failed banks and dates of failure based on FDIC data. To properly assess the predictive power of potential leading indicators during the present bank crisis, we developed a control group of healthy banks.

We used the Uniform Bank Performance Report to identify banks in the same general peer group and then selected two in the same state for each failed bank. For each failed thrift, we selected two thrifts from the same state as peers.

Econometric Results

We estimated a variety of four- and eight-quarter ahead forecasting models via logit using Huber-White robust standard errors. Technically, our estimates were based on five- and nine-quarter ahead forecasts because the Call Report data are released well after the dated quarter. For example, we used fourth-quarter 2006 data, available sometime during the first quarter of 2007, to determine if a bank failed in the second, third, or fourth quarter of 2007 or the first quarter of 2008.

We adopt in-sample measures of model and variable performance but no traditional test of out of sample forecasting ability (e.g., estimating the model through 2009 and measuring forecast accuracy in 2010). However, the logistic regressions can be thought of (with the exception of the concentration index) as an out-of-sample test of the models and variables as they were estimated in the aforementioned assessments of earlier waves of bank failures published 1995 and 1998.[4]

We first estimated a model with the five leading indicators identified previously, at four- and eight-quarter forecasting horizons. As evident in tables 7 and 8 below, these five indicators remain highly significant predictors of bank failure.

Table 7. Logit Model of Bank Failure with Standard Financial Ratios, Four-Quarter Horizon

Indicator	Coefficient	p-value
Capital	-36.4539	< 0.0001
Earnings	-46.8159	<0.0001
Nonperforming loans	27.9025	< 0.0001
Securities	-0.9936	0.0400
Unstable funding	1.0405	0.0103
McFadden's r-squared	0.47	Not applicable

Source: GAO analysis of data from FDIC and SNL Financial.

Table 8. Logit Model of Bank Failure with Standard Financial Ratios, Eight-Quarter Horizon

Indicator	Coefficient	p-value
Capital	-8.0321	< 0.0001
Earnings	-68.0782	< 0.0001
Nonperforming loans	42.3400	< 0.0001
Securities	-1.5070	< 0.0001
Unstable funding	1.2953	< 0.0001
McFadden's r-squared	0.22	Not applicable

Source: GAO analysis of data from FDIC and SNL Financial.

Next we estimated two models at a four-quarter horizon with our two measures of sector loan concentration in addition to the five indicators. As evident in tables 9 and 10 below, both concentration indices are significant predictors of bank failure, though the p-value of the coefficient estimate for HHI 2 is much smaller.

Table 9. Logit Model of Bank Failure with HHI 1, Four-Quarter Horizon

Indicator	Coefficient	p-value
Capital	-36.6820	< 0.0001
Earnings	-47.0561	< 0.0001
Nonperforming loans	27.6294	< 0.0001
Securities	-0.8334	0.0820
Unstable funding	1.0163	0.0111
HHI 1	0.0001	0.0124
McFadden's r-squared	0.47	Not applicable

Source: GAO analysis of data from FDIC and SNL Financial.

Table 10. Logit Model of Bank Failure with HHI 2, Four-Quarter Horizon

Indicator	Coefficient	p-value
Capital	-37.2551	< 0.0001
Earnings	-47.0610	< 0.0001
Nonperforming loans	27.4433	< 0.0001
Securities	-0.7846	0.0916
Unstable funding	0.8846	0.0276
HHI 2	0.0002	< 0.0001
McFadden's r-squared	0.47	Not applicable

Source: GAO analysis of data from FDIC and SNL Financial.

We estimated marginal effects of one-standard deviation changes based on the coefficients in table 10. The magnitude or practical significance of these indicators is also notable, with a one-standard deviation increase in the indicator changing the probability of failure over the next year (from about 2.8 percent at the means of the independent variables) in the next four quarters as follows:[5]

- capital: down 2.7 percentage points,
- earnings: down 0.7 percentage points,
- nonperforming loans: up 5.0 percentage points,
- securities: down 0.5 percentage points,
- unstable funding: up 0.3 percentage points,
- concentration index: up 0.9 percentage points.

It is possible that the concentration index is predictive of failure because many failed banks had loan concentrations in sectors that experienced downturns, not because the institutions were less diversified overall. Concentration in the CRE sector in particular could explain the predictive power of the concentration index because of the recent downturn in CRE.

As evident in tables 11 and 12 below, while CRE is predictive of bank failure, HHI 2 remains predictive after controlling for CRE concentration, though the coefficient is smaller and less significant than the model in table 10.

**Table 11. Logit Model of Bank Failure with CRE,
Four-Quarter Horizon**

Indicator	Coefficient	p-value
Capital	-39.0898	< 0.0001
Earnings	-46.7415	< 0.0001
Nonperforming loans	26.5067	< 0.0001
Securities	-1.0568	0.0351
Unstable funding	0.3991	0.3722
CRE	0.0133	< 0.0001
McFadden's r-squared	0.47	Not applicable

Source: GAO analysis of data from FDIC and SNL Financial.

**Table 12. Logit Model of Bank Failure with CRE and HHI 2,
Four-Quarter Horizon**

Indicator	Coefficient	p-value
Capital	-39.0078	< 0.0001
Earnings	-46.9419	< 0.0001
Nonperforming loans	26.5317	< 0.0001
Securities	-0.8993	0.0672
Unstable funding	0.4153	0.3486
CRE	0.0099	0.0001
HHI 2	0.0001	0.0013
McFadden's r-squared	0.48	Not applicable

Source: GAO analysis of data from FDIC and SNL Financial.

Next we estimated a model with HHI 2 at the eight-quarter horizon. As evident in table 13, the concentration index remained a statistically significant predictor at the longer horizon. Next we estimated a model with only CAMELS ratings at four- and eight-quarter horizons, along with a model combining CAMELS ratings with the model in table 10 (five indicators plus HHI 2) also at four- and eight-quarter horizons.

Table 13. Logit Model of Bank Failure with HHI 2, Eight-Quarter Horizon

Indicator	Coefficient	p-value
Capital	-9.4549	< 0.0001
Earnings	-69.9422	< 0.0001
Nonperforming loans	42.5927	< 0.0001
Securities	-1.1304	0.0003
Unstable funding	0.9810	0.0001
HHI 2	0.0002	< 0.0001
McFadden's r-squared	0.24	Not applicable

Source: GAO analysis of data from FDIC and SNL Financial.

As evident in tables 14-17, CAMELS ratings on their own are predictive of bank failure within four and eight quarters. As a composite index meant to capture the underlying CAMELS component factors (capital, asset quality, management, earnings, liquidity, and sensitivity to market risk) CAMELS are similar to a predictive regression model based on financial indicators that represent some of those categories—in the sense that they both take into account more than just capital. However, CAMELS ratings have less explanatory power by themselves, as measured by McFadden's r-squared, 0.26 versus 0.47 for the logit with the financial ratios and concentration index. Furthermore, CAMELS ratings and the financial ratios we have chosen each contain unique information that can be helpful in anticipating bank distress. CAMELS ratings remain a highly statistically significant predictor of bank failure when added to a regression with capital, earnings, nonperforming loans, securities, unstable funding, and the concentration index, though unsurprisingly the coefficient is somewhat less significant than on its own. Thus CAMELS ratings contain information that is not fully accounted for by the financial indicators we have identified and included in the regression, and vice versa.

Finally, we estimated marginal effect of a one-rating increase (deterioration) in the CAMELS rating based on the coefficients in table 15. The magnitude or practical significance of the CAMELS rating is also notable, with a one-rating increase changing the probability of failure over the next year from about 2.8 percent to 4.2 percent.[6]

Table 14. Logit Model of Bank Failure with CAMELS, Four-Quarter Horizon

Indicator	Coefficient	p-value
CAMELS rating	1.5649	< 0.0001
McFadden's r-squared	0.26	Not applicable

Source: GAO analysis of data from FDIC and SNL Financial.

Table 15. Logit Model of Bank Failure with CAMELS, Eight-Quarter Horizon

Indicator	Coefficient	p-value
CAMELS rating	1.0279	< 0.0001
McFadden's r-squared	0.08	Not applicable

Source: GAO analysis of data from FDIC and SNL Financial.

Table 16. Logit Model of Bank Failure with CAMELS and Financial Indicators, Four-Quarter Horizon

Indicator	Coefficient	p-value
Capital	-34.2274	< 0.0001
Earnings	-44.3722	< 0.0001
Nonperforming loans	23.2022	< 0.0001
Securities	-0.7588	0.1072
Unstable funding	1.0172	0.0101
HHI 2	0.0002	< 0.0001
CAMELS rating	0.4250	< 0.0001
McFadden's r-squared	0.48	Not applicable

Source: GAO analysis of data from FDIC and SNL Financial.

Table 17. Logit Model of Bank Failure with CAMELS and Financial Indicators, Eight-Quarter Horizon

Indicator	Coefficient	p-value
Capital	-10.6895	< 0.0001
Earnings	-57.7312	< 0.0001
Nonperforming loans	40.5932	< 0.0001
Securities	-1.1024	0.0005
Unstable funding	0.9770	0.0001
HHI 2	0.0002	< 0.0001
CAMELS rating	0.2834	0.0002
McFadden's r-squared	0.25	Not applicable

Source: GAO analysis of data from FDIC and SNL Financial.

Analysis of DIF Losses

We estimated a variety of econometric models to assess the impact of PCA on the DIF. Our model includes all bank failures from first quarter 2007 to third quarter 2010. In order to derive a better estimate of PCA's impact than comparing mean or median losses, we controlled for other factors that might affect losses to the DIF and therefore account for some systematic differences between banks that underwent the PCA process before failure and those that did not. We attempted to control for factors related to the quality of the bank's balance sheet (and therefore expected value to potential buyers) and the size of FDIC's deposit liabilities.[7]

We report on the results of several models we estimated via ordinary least-squares (OLS) below. All models reported below were estimated with White standard errors. Prompt corrective action is a dummy variable equal to "1" if the failed institution underwent the PCA process, "0" otherwise.

While PCA was not statistically significant in any of the specifications we ran, it was consistently negative in the 1-3 percentage point range.[8] Because institutions that underwent PCA had on average almost $1 billion in assets, a small effect that did not meet conventional standards for statistical significance might in some circumstances be of practical or economic significance.[9]

Table 18. Potential Factors Affecting DIF Losses

Control variable	Definition	Explanation
Deposits	Several measures of deposits divided by assets.	Measures FDIC liabilities.
Securities	Securities divided by assets	Securities are generally more liquid and therefore easier to value.
Nonperforming loans or assets	Nonperforming loans are the sum of past due loans, nonaccrual loans, and real estate owned divided by assets; nonperforming assets also include nonloan assets that are repossessed or in nonaccrual status	Measures the quality of loans or assets that may have limited value outside the depository institution, and therefore low resale value.

Source: GAO.

Mean losses for PCA versus non-PCA banks are 28 percent of assets versus 25.6 percent of assets (the difference was not statistically significant) before controlling for other factors. After controlling for other factors, banks that underwent the PCA process had 1-3 percentage point lower losses as a percentage of assets, though the difference remained statistically insignificant. In total, controlling for balance sheet quality resulted in a roughly 3-5 point change in DIF losses and suggests a more positive role for PCA in reducing losses to the DIF. In addition, the balance sheet factors are all highly statistically significant.

As shown in table 19, in the model with deposits measured as the total deposits of the bank (which may exceed the liabilities of the FDIC), the coefficient on PCA was roughly negative 3—banks that underwent PCA had DIF losses that were roughly 3 percentage points less as a percentage of assets—but not statistically significant.

Table 19. Model of DIF Losses with Nonperforming Loans and Total Deposits, First Quarter 2007–Third Quarter 2010

Variable	Coefficient	p-value
Securities	-0.1626	0.0615
Nonperforming loans	0.3628	0.0001
Deposits	0.3909	< 0.0001
PCA	-3.1609	0.2397
R-squared	0.21	Not applicable

Source: GAO analysis of data from FDIC and SNL Financial.

Table 20. Model of DIF Losses with Nonperforming Loans and Small Deposits, First Quarter 2007–Third Quarter 2010

Variable	Coefficient	p-value
Securities	-0.2096	0.0105
Nonperforming loans	0.4653	< 0.0001
Small deposits	0.2707	< 0.0001
PCA	-1.1196	0.6596
R-squared	0.21	Not applicable

Source: GAO analysis of data from FDIC and SNL Financial.

Table 21. Model of DIF Losses with Nonperforming Assets and Small Deposits, First Quarter 2007–Third Quarter 2010

Variable	Coefficient	p-value
Securities	-0.2170	0.0077
Nonperforming loans	0.4426	< 0.0001
Small deposits	0.2726	< 0.0001
PCA	-1.1627	0.6480
R-squared	0.23	Not applicable

Source: GAO analysis of data from FDIC and SNL Financial.

As shown in table 20, in the model with deposits measured as the small deposits of the bank (which may understate the liabilities of the FDIC), the coefficient on PCA was roughly negative 1—banks that underwent PCA had DIF losses that were roughly 1 percentage point less as a percentage of assets—but not statistically significant.

As shown in table 21, in the model with deposits measured as the small deposits of the bank and nonperforming assets substituted for nonperforming loans, in table 20, the coefficient on PCA was also roughly negative 1—banks that underwent PCA had DIF losses that were roughly 1 percentage point less as a percentage of assets—but not statistically significant.

APPENDIX IV: PCA SURVEY RESPONDENTS

We asked 44 informed stakeholders from the regulatory, research, and industry sectors to complete our first and second surveys about prompt corrective action. For more information on our survey and selection methodologies, see appendix I. The following table lists the individuals from whom we received completed responses to the first, second, or both surveys.

Table 22. Survey Respondents

Name	Primary organization
Braswell, Rob	Georgia Department of Banking and Finance
Clarke, Scott	Illinois Department of Financial and Professional Regulations
Cole, Chris	Independent Community Bankers of America

Table 22. (Continued)

Name	Primary organization
Corcoran, Kevin	OTS
Douglas, John	Davis Polk and Wardwell LLC
Duffie, Darrell	Stanford University
Eisenbeis, Robert A.	Cumberland Advisors
Ellis, Diane	FDIC, Financial Risk Management and Research, Division ofInsurance and Research
Evanoff, Douglas D.	Federal Reserve Bank of Chicago
Gerrish, Jeff	Gerrish McCreary Smith Consultants and Attorneys
Grace, Ray	North Carolina Commissioner of Banks
Hancock, Diana	Federal Reserve, Division of Research and Statistics
Ivie, Stan	FDIC, Division of Supervision and Consumer Protection
Kane, Edward J.	Boston College
Kaufman, George	Loyola University, Graduate School of Business
Kelly, Jennifer	OCC, Division of Midsize/Community Bank Supervision
Lemieux, Cathy	Federal Reserve Bank of Chicago
Leuz, Christian	University of Chicago
Levonian, Mark	OCC
Litan, Robert E.	Brookings Institution
Loving, Bill	Pendleton Bank
Nieto, Maria	Bank of Spain
Oakes, Nancy	Federal Reserve, Enforcement
Quigley, Lori	OTS
Scott, Kenneth E.	Stanford University
Spoth, Christopher J.	FDIC, Division of Supervision and Consumer Protection
Stevens, Michael	Conference of State Bank Supervisors
Sweeney, Maureen	FDIC, Division of Insurance and Research
Tenhundfeld, Mark	America Bankers Association
Thompson, Sandra L.	FDIC, Division of Supervision and Consumer Protection
Wall, Larry	Federal Reserve Bank of Atlanta
Watkins, Rick	Federal Reserve, Supervisory Issues and Special Situations

Source: GAO.

APPENDIX V: RESPONSES TO QUESTIONS FROM GAO'S SECOND DELPHI SURVEY ON THE PROMPT CORRECTIVE ACTION FRAMEWORK

We distributed a survey to 44 individuals from the regulatory, research, and industry sectors to determine their views on the PCA framework and options for modifying the PCA framework to minimize losses to the DIF. We received completed responses from 29 of 44 individuals, for a response rate of 66 percent.

Tables 23-28 and figures 17-18 below show responses to questions from the survey. For more information about our methodology for designing and distributing the survey, see appendix I.

Section 1: PCA Positive Elements and Shortcomings

Table 23. Stakeholder Views on Potential Positive Elements of the PCA Framework

Stakeholder views	Positive element of PCA	Not a positive element of PCA	No opinion	Total
Establishes consistent capital standards and corresponding restrictions and requirements	24	3	1	28
Gives institutions an incentive to avoid or resolve capital deficiencies	27	1	0	28
Makes institutions less likely to fail	16	10	2	28
Helps reduce regulatory forbearance	16	9	3	28
Helps close institutions before insolvency (i.e., before they develop negative net worth)	23	3	2	28

Source: GAO.

Note: Totals may not add to 29 because respondents did not all answer every question.

**Table 24. Stakeholder Views on Potential Shortcomings
of the PCA Framework**

Stakeholder views	Shortcoming of PCA	Not a shortcoming of PCA	No opinion	Total
Capital is a lagging indicator.	22	6	0	28
The measurement of capital is subjective (e.g., loan loss reserves may be insufficient, financial reporting may be inaccurate, etc.).	23	5	0	28
The focus of PCA is too narrow (e.g., it is based only on capital; it applies only to institutions, not holding companies, etc.).	22	5	1	28
PCA restrictions and requirements have limited flexibility.	13	15	0	28
During times of severe economic stress, PCA's effectiveness is more limited.	22	2	4	28

Source: GAO.

Note: Totals may not add to 29 because all respondents did not answer every question.

Section 2: Rating Options to Modify the PCA Framework

**Table 25. Stakeholder Views on Potential Impact of Each Option to Make
the PCA Framework More Effective in Minimizing Losses to the DIF**

Stakeholder views	Would diminish effectiveness	No impact	Would improve effectiveness	Unsure	Total
Change accounting rules used to measure capital levels (e.g., make greater use of market values to assess assets, change rules for loan loss reserves, etc.)	7	1	14	7	29

Stakeholder views	Would diminish effectiveness	No impact	Would improve effectiveness	Unsure	Total
Eliminate the PCA framework	22	2	2	3	29
Encourage greater uniformity across regulators (e.g., more consistency in capital definitions across state regulators and in closure authority across federal regulators, etc.)	2	5	21	1	29
Enhance restrictions and requirements at the holding company level	1	5	18	5	29
Include another trigger for PCA (i.e., another measure of bank soundness or performance)	1	2	18	8	29
Incorporate an institution's risk profile (e.g., concentration exposure, etc.) into the PCA capital category thresholds	2	2	21	4	29
Make no changes to the PCA framework	13	13	0	3	29
Make PCA restrictions and requirements less prescriptive (e.g., more flexibility in timelines, more discretion in application of restrictions, etc.)	15	2	8	4	29
Raise all capital category thresholds	4	3	17	5	29
Raise capital category thresholds for larger institutions	2	6	15	5	28
Raise the critically undercapitalized threshold	3	5	20	1	29
Strengthen PCA restrictions and requirements (e.g., shorter time frames, earlier use of restrictions available under the significantly undercapitalized category, etc.)	8	1	15	5	29

Source: GAO.

Note: Totals may not add to 29 because respondents did not all answer every question.

Table 26. Stakeholder Views on Potential Feasibility for Federal Regulators to Implement Each Option

Stakeholder views	Feasible	Not Feasible	Unsure	Total
Change accounting rules used to measure capital levels (e.g., make greater use of market values to assess assets, change rules for loan loss reserves, etc.)	13	6	10	29
Eliminate the PCA framework	5	14	10	29
Encourage greater uniformity across regulators (e.g., more consistency in capital definitions across state regulators and in closure authority across federal regulators, etc.)	16	2	11	29
Enhance restrictions and requirements at the holding company level	19	2	8	29
Include another trigger for PCA (i.e., another measure of bank soundness or performance)	20	3	6	29
Incorporate an institution's risk profile (e.g., concentration exposure, etc.) into the PCA capital category thresholds	22	1	6	29
Make PCA restrictions and requirements less prescriptive (e.g., more flexibility in timelines, more discretion in application of restrictions, etc.)	16	4	9	29
Raise all capital category thresholds	17	6	6	29
Raise capital category thresholds for larger institutions	18	1	9	28
Raise the critically undercapitalized threshold	20	4	5	29
Strengthen PCA restrictions and requirements (e.g., shorter time frames, earlier use of restrictions available under the significantly undercapitalized category, etc.)	16	6	7	29

Source: GAO.

Note: Totals may not add to 29 because respondents did not all answer every question.

Section 3: Rank Ordering of Options to Modify the PCA Framework

Table 27. Stakeholder Ranking of 12 Potential Options to Modify PCA

Potential options	Most effective option	Second most effective option	Third most effective option	Total number of respondents selecting option among top three most effective
Change accounting rules used to measure capital levels (e.g., make greater use of market values to assess assets, change rules for loan loss reserves, etc.)	3	3	1	7
Eliminate the PCA framework	1	0	1	2
Encourage greater uniformity across regulators (e.g., more consistency in capital definitions across state regulators and in closure authority across federal regulators, etc.)	0	3	5	8
Enhance restrictions and requirements at the holding company level	3	2	3	8
Include another trigger for PCA (i.e., another measure of bank soundness or performance)	3	4	5	12
Incorporate an institution's risk profile (e.g., concentration exposure, etc.) into the PCA capital category thresholds	5	6	1	12
Make no changes to PCA framework	0	0	0	0
Make PCA restrictions and requirements less prescriptive (e.g., more flexibility in timelines, more discretion in application of restrictions, etc.)	4	1	1	6

Table 27. (Continued)

Potential options	Most effective option	Second most effective option	Third most effective option	Total number of respondents selecting option among top three most effective
Raise all capital category thresholds	7	2	1	10
Raise capital category thresholds for larger institutions	0	3	2	5
Raise the critically undercapitalized threshold	2	3	3	8
Strengthen PCA restrictions and requirements (e.g., shorter timeframes, earlier use of restrictions available under the significantly undercapitalized category, etc.)	0	1	2	3
Total	28	28	25	

Source: GAO.

Note: Totals may not add to 29 because respondents did not all answer every question.

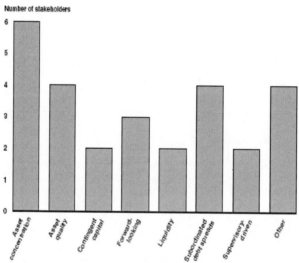

Note: Total may not add to 29 because respondents did not all answer every question.
    Stakeholders.

Source: GAO analysis of FDIC data.

Figure 17. Stakeholder Views on Potential Additional PCA Trigger That Would Have the Most Positive Impact on PCA Effectiveness.

Table 28. Stakeholder Views on the Potential Impact of Potential Additional PCA Triggers

Potential additional triggers	Would diminish effectiveness of PCA	No impact	Would improve effectiveness of PCA	Unsure	Total
Asset concentration trigger	4	1	20	4	29
Asset quality trigger (e.g., nonperforming assets, etc.)	1	0	26	1	28
Contingent capital trigger	3	3	10	13	29
Forward-looking trigger (e.g., stress test results, etc.)	2	1	13	12	28
Liquidity trigger	4	2	19	4	29
Sources of funding trigger (e.g., level of brokered deposits, mismatch between short-term funding and long-term lending, etc.)	6	2	16	5	29
Subordinated debt spreads trigger	1	2	14	12	29
Supervisory-driven trigger (e.g., CAMELS ratings, etc.)	5	3	14	7	29

Source: GAO.

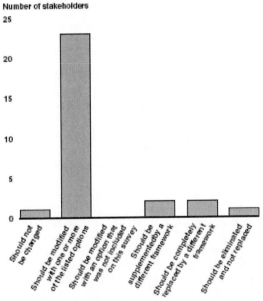

Source: GAO analysis of FDIC data.

Note: Total may not add to 29 because respondents did not all answer every question.

Figure 18. Stakeholder Overall Opinion of the PCA Framework.

End Notes

[1] The DIF was created in 2006, when the Federal Deposit Insurance Reform Act of 2005 provided for the merging of the Bank Insurance Fund and the Saving Association Insurance Fund. Pub. L. No. 109-171, title II, subtitle B, § 2102, 120 Stat. 4 (2006). The Federal Deposit Insurance Corporation (FDIC) administers the DIF, the goal of which is to (1) insure the deposits and protect the depositors of DIF-insured institutions, and (2) upon appointment of FDIC as receiver, resolve failed DIF-insured institutions at the least possible cost to the DIF (unless a systemic risk determination is made). The DIF is primarily funded from deposit insurance assessments.

[2] Pub. L. No. 102-242, 105 Stat. 2236 (1991); Ch. 967, §§ 1,2, 64 Stat. 873 (1950).

[3] 12 U.S.C. § 1831o.

[4] 12 U.S.C. § 1831p-1.

[5] See GAO, Troubled Asset Relief Program: Additional Actions Needed to Better Ensure Integrity, Accountability, and Transparency, GAO-09-161 (Washington D.C.: Dec. 2, 2008).

[6] See GAO, Federal Deposit Insurance Act: Regulators' Use of Systemic Risk Exception Raises Moral Hazard Concerns and Opportunities Exist to Clarify the Provision, GAO-10-100 (Washington, D.C.: Apr. 15, 2010).

[7] 12 U.S.C. § 5382(g). The Financial Stability Oversight Council (FSOC) was created by the Dodd-Frank Act to provide comprehensive monitoring to ensure the stability of the nation's financial system and has responsibilities to facilitate coordination among the member agencies, recommend stricter standards if necessary, and make recommendations to Congress in closing specific regulatory gaps. Voting members include, among others, the Secretary of the Treasury, who serves as the Chairperson of FSOC; the Chairman of the Board of Governors of the Federal Reserve System; the Comptroller of the Currency; and the Chairperson of FDIC. 12 U.S.C. § 5321.

[8] This report uses the phrase "banks that underwent the PCA process" to describe banks that fell into one of the three lowest PCA capital thresholds—undercapitalized, significantly undercapitalized, or critically undercapitalized—during any quarter in our period of analysis.

[9] We reported in March 2011 that FDIC maintained effective internal control over financial statements for the DIF. GAO, Financial Audit: Federal Deposit Insurance Corporation Funds' 2010 and 2009 Financial Statements, GAO-11-412 (Washington, D.C.: Mar. 18, 2011).

[10] Section 313 of the Dodd-Frank Act abolishes OTS and section 312 distributes its regulatory functions among the Federal Reserve, FDIC, and OCC. OTS will cease to exist 90 days after the transfer date, which is July 21, 2011, unless it is extended to another date that is within 18 months of July 21, 2010. See 12 U.S.C. §§ 5411-13.

[11] In October 2008, the standard maximum insurance amount of $100,000 was temporarily raised to $250,000, effective through December 31, 2013. See 12 U.S.C. § 5241. Section 335(a)(1) of the Dodd-Frank Act, signed into law on July 21, 2010, made this increase permanent. See 12 U.S.C. 1821(a)(1)(E).

[12] 12 U.S.C. § 1818.

[13] 12 U.S.C. § 1831o(c).

[14] Section 38 allows an exception to the 90-day closure rule if both the primary regulator and FDIC concur and document why some other action would better achieve the purpose of

section 38—resolving the problems of institutions at the least possible long-term cost to the DIF.

[15] A bank can be reclassified or downgraded to critically undercapitalized only based on its failure to maintain a tangible equity to total assets ratio of at least 2 percent.

[16] See GAO, Deposit Insurance: Assessment of Regulators' Use of Prompt Corrective Action Provisions and FDIC's New Deposit Insurance System, GAO-07-242 (Washington, D.C.: Feb. 15, 2007).

[17] Capital levels, reported by institutions through Call and Thrift Financial Reports, may drop precipitously from previously reported levels, including conditions prompting liquidity issues, necessitating the closing of a bank without an opportunity to pursue PCA measures prior to failure.

[18] Many of these banks were merged into an acquiring bank without financial assistance from the government, although some were merged with governmental assistance or were dissolved through a voluntary liquidation that did not result in a new institution. These 46 dissolved banks are now classified as inactive by FDIC, although components of these banks may operate under the certification number of an acquiring bank. We did not count as dissolved 253 banks that continued to operate under their original unique certification number and were classified as active by FDIC, regardless of whether another entity had gained a large or controlling stake in their operations.

[19] Expressed as means, the average loss was 28.0 percent of assets for banks that underwent the PCA process; for banks that did not, the average loss was 25.6 percent. This report frequently uses medians when calculating averages so that the results are less sensitive to values at the extremes of the sample. For example, median losses divide banks into equal groups, half with losses above that amount, and half with losses below it.

[20] Statistical significance refers to the likelihood of an observed difference being due to chance. We controlled for factors affecting the quality of the balance sheet and the size of deposit liabilities. Banks with more securities had lower losses, and banks with more nonperforming loans and deposits had higher losses. See appendix III for more information.

[21] Expressed as means, the average size of the 25 banks that did not undergo the PCA process before failure was $14.8 billion, versus $956 million for those banks that first underwent the PCA process. If we exclude Washington Mutual Bank, or WaMu—the nation's largest savings and loan association before its failure—the mean size of banks that did not undergo the PCA process before failure drops from $14.8 billion to $2.6 billion.

[22] In this report, we use the term "forbearance" to refer to granting banks temporary relief from compliance with regulatory requirements.

[23] See 12 C.F.R. § 337.6.

[24] For example, some large institutions did not fail but received other assistance authorized under systemic risk determinations related to (1) the banking system as a whole through the Temporary Liquidity Guarantee Facility; and (2) Citigroup and its insured institution subsidiaries. See GAO-10-100 for further information on the use of systemic risk determinations.

[25] Joe Peek and Eric Rosengren, "The Use of Capital Ratios to Trigger Interventions in Problem Banks: Too Little, Too Late," New England Economic Review, September/October issue (1996).

[26] David S. Jones and Kathleen Kuester King, "The Implementation of Prompt Corrective Action: An Assessment," Journal of Banking and Finance, vol.19 (1995).

[27] GAO, Bank Supervision: Prompt and Forceful Regulatory Actions Needed, GAO/GGD-91-69 (Washington, D.C.: April 1991).

[28] A composite indicator is an indicator that integrates information from a number of distinct indicators.

[29] We relied on two widely cited studies. See Rebel A. Cole and Jeffrey W. Gunther, "Separating the Likelihood and Timing of Bank Failure," Journal of Banking and Finance, vol.19 (1995) and Rebel A. Cole and Jeffrey W. Gunther, "Predicting Bank Failure: A Comparison of On- and Off-site Monitoring Systems," Journal of Financial Services Research, vol.13, no.2 (1998).

[30] In contrast to statistical significance, which refers to the likelihood of an observed difference being due to chance, practical significance refers to the magnitude of an observed difference.

[31] See Basel Committee on Banking Supervision, Basel III: International Framework for Liquidity Risk Measurement, Standards, and Monitoring. December 2010. Basel, Switzerland.

[32] We measure sector loan concentration as a Herfindahl-Hirschman Index (HHI) where the "market shares" are the proportion of loans in each sector. See appendix III for more information.

[33] John O'Keefe and James A. Wilcox, "How Has Bank Supervision Performed and How Might It Be Improved?" Paper presented at Federal Reserve Bank of Boston's 54th Economic Conference "After the Fall: Re-Evaluating Supervisory, Regulatory, and Monetary Policy" (2009).

[34] FDIC's Statistical CAMELS Off-site Rating (SCOR) system was designed to help the agency identify institutions that have experienced noticeable financial deterioration. The model helps predict 1- and 2-rated institutions in danger of being downgraded to 3 or worse. The Federal Reserve uses the Supervision and Regulation Statistical Assessment of Bank Risk model (SR-SABR) as its primary off-site monitoring tool.

[35] To assess the prevalence of failed banks that previously had been identified on the regulators' watch or review lists, we assessed 252 banks regulated by FDIC, the Federal Reserve, and OCC that failed from the first quarter of 2008 through the third quarter of 2010. We identified when the banks were included on the regulators' watch or review lists within 2 years of their failure. OTS also conducts off-site monitoring to identify institutions that warrant further scrutiny that are captured in a high risk profile list. Because of some complications in collecting these data for the entire time period of our analysis, we did not include OTS institutions in this analysis.

[36] Uniform Financial Institution Rating System, 62 Fed. Reg. 752 (Jan. 6, 1997).

[37] We reviewed CAMELS ratings over a 2-year period prior to bank failure for 292 banks that failed from the first quarter of 2008 through the third quarter of 2010.

[38] Through a systematic review of material loss reviews or other evaluations performed on 136 institutions that failed between in 2008, 2009, and 2010, we identified the first enforcement action relevant to the regulator's efforts to address deteriorating conditions in banks in the 2-year period before failure.

[39] GAO, Deposit Insurance: A Strategy for Reform, GAO/GGD-91-26 (Washington, D.C.: March 1991), and GAO/GGD-91-69.

[40] A de novo bank is a newly chartered bank that has been open for less than 3 years.

[41] Of the remaining six respondents, two said PCA should be supplemented by a different framework, two said PCA should be completely replaced by a different framework, one told us PCA should be eliminated and not replaced, and one stakeholder told us the PCA framework should not be changed.

[42] Of the remaining eight, two survey respondents said incorporating an institution's risk profile into the PCA capital category thresholds would have no impact, two told us it would diminish the effectiveness of PCA, and four were unsure.

[43] To categorize institutions into the five PCA capital categories, two capital measures (total risk-based capital ratio and Tier 1 risk-based capital ratio) divide the amount of capital by risk-weighted assets.

[44] Of the remaining 12, 3 told us raising all capital category thresholds would have no impact, 4 said it would diminish PCA effectiveness, and 5 respondents were unsure.

[45] See 57 Fed. Reg. 44866 (Sept. 29, 1992).

[46] GAO, Risk-Based Capital: Bank Regulators Need to Improve Transparency and Overcome Impediments to Finalizing the Proposed Basel II Framework, GAO-07-253 (Washington, D.C.: Feb. 15, 2007); Congressional Research Service, Who Regulates Whom? An Overview of U.S. Fiscal Supervision, R40249 (Washington, D.C.: Dec. 8, 2010).

[47] See Who Regulates Whom; GAO-07-253; Douglass Elliott, "A Primer on Bank Capital" The Brookings Institution. (Washington, D.C.: Jan. 28, 2010).

[48] Of the remaining 11, 1 said adding another PCA trigger would diminish PCA effectiveness, 2 told us it would have no impact, and 8 were unsure.

[49] One survey respondent did not answer this question; therefore, the total number of respondents in this case is 28.

[50] Pub. L. No. 103-325, § 318, 18 Stat. 2160, 2223-2224 (1994) (providing for the standards to be issued either by regulation [as originally specified in FDICIA] or by guideline and eliminating the requirement to establish quantitative standards for asset quality and earnings).

[51] GAO, Bank and Thrift Regulation: Implementation of FDICIA's Prompt Regulatory Action Provisions, GAO/GGD-97-18 (Washington, D.C.: Nov. 21, 1996).

[52] GAO-07-242.

[53] GAO-07-242, GAO/GGD-97-18, and GAO/GGD-91-69.

[54] GAO/GGD-91-69 and GAO/GGD-91-26.

End Note for Appendix II

[1] 12 U.S.C. § 1823(c)(4).

End Notes for Appendix III

[1] Cole and Gunther, "Separating the Likelihood and Timing of Bank Failure," and Cole and Gunther, "Predicting Bank Failure: A Comparison of On- and Off-site Monitoring Systems."

[2] Basel Committee on Banking Supervision, Studies on Credit Risk Concentration. Working Paper No. 15, November, 2006. Basel, Switzerland. Deutsche Bundesbank, Concentration Risk in Credit Portfolios. Monthly Report, June 2006. Frankfurt, Germany.

[3] Office of the Comptroller of the Currency, Board of Governors of the Federal Reserve System, Federal Deposit Insurance Corporation, Concentrations in Commercial Real Estate Lending, Sound Risk Management Practices, December, 2006.

[4] Cole and Gunther, "Separating the Likelihood and Timing of Bank Failure," and Cole and Gunther, "Predicting Bank Failure: A Comparison of On- and Off-site Monitoring Systems."

[5] The marginal effect is calculated at the means of the independent variables in the first quarter of 2008.

[6] As above, the marginal effect is calculated at the means of the independent variables in the first quarter of 2008. For comparison purposes, a one standard deviation (0.7) increase in the CAMELS rating raises the probability of failure by 0.9 percentage points, to 3.7 percent.

[7] A similar approach that is not focused on the effect of PCA is Kathleen McDill, "Resolution Costs and the Business Cycle," FDIC Working Paper 2004-01 (2004).

[8] While in theory DIF losses are a random variable that could take on positive or negative (if the FDIC turned a profit on the sale of a failed bank) values, the FDIC has not earned profits over its deposit liabilities on any bank resolution. Therefore, one might consider the dependent variable to be censored and a regression approach such as a Tobit might be appropriate. For each of the OLS regressions reported below we performed the regressions again as a Tobit to see if our results were sensitive to this specification. We did not find any substantive changes as the coefficient on PCA remained statistically insignificant and in the negative 1-3 range.

[9] See, e.g., Deirdre N. McCloskey and Stephen T. Ziliak, "The Standard Error of Regressions," Journal of Economic Literature (1996).

INDEX